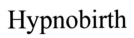

Hypnobirth

Hypnobirth

Theories and Practices for Healthcare Professionals

Yulia Watters, PhD

ROWMAN & LITTLEFIELD
Lanham • Boulder • New York • London

Published by Rowman & Littlefield
A wholly owned subsidiary of The Rowman & Littlefield Publishing Group, Inc.
4501 Forbes Boulevard, Suite 200, Lanham, Maryland 20706
www.rowman.com

Unit A, Whitacre Mews, 26-34 Stannary Street, London SE11 4AB

British Library Cataloguing in Publication Information Available

Library of Congress Cataloging-in-Publication Data

Watters, Yulia, author.
Hypnobirth : theories and practices for healthcare professionals / Yulia Watters.
p. ; cm.
Includes bibliographical references and index.
ISBN 978-1-4422-3704-9 (cloth : alk. paper) -- ISBN 978-1-4422-3706-3 (electronic)
I. Title.
[DNLM: 1. Hypnosis. 2. Parturition. 3. Pregnancy. WM 415]
RG525
618.2--dc23
2014046827

Printed in the United States of America

To my daughter, Allyson.

Contents

Foreword

I have written three books about hypnosis and its use to help relieve suffering in psychotherapy settings.

But like many, before I learned hypnosis and what it is really all about I had two contradictory attitudes toward it:

1. I was curious, perhaps even fascinated, by hypnosis. What was it all about? Could I be hypnotized? Could I be controlled by hypnosis? Could it help me?

And, 2. I was frightened and wary of hypnosis. I didn't want to be controlled by someone else. I was concerned that I would go to a hypnotist and he (it always seemed to be a "he" in my fearful imaginings, a fellow with a goatee and mesmerizing eyes) would tell me to come back each week and pay him a princely fee I could scarce afford, and then to forget he had given me this suggestion.

When I finally experienced hypnosis, it was much different from what I had expected. More gentle, more empowering rather than controlling.

I felt more free, more in touch with possibilities than I had imagined I would.

I could hear and understand everything the hypnotist said while I was in trance. (I had expected to be "knocked out" in some way, I suppose.)

More than that, I was able to make significant changes more easily than I thought possible.

It did help that the person who first hypnotized me was one of the premier medical hypnotists of the twentieth century, Dr. Milton H. Erickson. Dr. Erickson, a psychiatrist, was a pioneer in exploring the possibilities of hypnosis for therapeutic purposes and was instrumental in getting it to be an approved tool for medical and psychotherapeutic practitioners.

Dr. Yulia Watters carries on in this Ericksonian tradition in several ways:

1. She is a committed researcher;

2. She uses a permissive, empowering, relational rather than authoritarian and controlling approach to hypnosis;

3. She is pioneering a new approach to using the hypnotic framework to the birth process, introducing medical practitioners to a new tool that can lead to better outcomes and lessen suffering in their patients.

This book can help any dedicated medical practitioner become more open, skilled, and knowledgeable about the powerful tool that is hypnosis, but more than that, it can help any medical practitioner (or therapist) shift their view of hypnosis radically from that old, fearful image to a new, relationship-based, permissive, and empowering image.

You will find in this book not only a solid summary of the history of hypnosis and the evidence that supports its use, but a clear guide to using hypnosis in your practice and medical setting.

One of the things that may stand out for you in reading *Hypnobirth* is the breadth and depth of the author's understandings and her use of various perspectives in understanding the experience of the person giving birth. This is no accident: Dr. Watters speaks three languages fluently and has lived in at least three different cultures for significant periods of her life. She is a practitioner, a researcher, and a scholar. She has worked with people giving birth, taught practitioners how to work with them using the hypnotic framework, and has given birth using the hypnotic tools she writes about in this book.

In other words, Dr. Watters is our best guide to using hypnosis to deepen connections between the mind and the body, between the practitioner and the patient, and between the practitioner and his or her creative self.

The thing that stands out for me in this new approach to hypnosis that Dr. Watters puts forth is that the person with whom we work hypnotically already has the answers and capabilities needed to have a more healthy and comfortable relationship to the pregnancy, labor, birth, and post-birth experience.

Just another note: I used hypnosis with my wife during the birth of our son in the 1980s. She had already mastered the Lamaze method of breathing and combining it with her previous hypnotic experience, hypnosis helped in the process, and created a nice collaborative, connective experience for us in the labor and birth process. Looking at the literature after this experience, I was surprised to find little on the subject of birth and labor, except for minimizing labor pains. There is clearly much more to this subject and *Hypnobirth* brings us that richness.

May this book help birth a new skill and a new phase in your professional work, one characterized by an increase in your confidence and effectiveness and in better and more meaningful connections to the people with whom you work.

And without belaboring the point any longer, let me pass you on to Dr. Yulia Watters and *Hypnobirth*.

Bill O'Hanlon
Santa Fe, New Mexico
November 2014

Preface

I was first introduced to hypnosis in graduate school. I was amazed at the incredible potential of this approach to treatment and, overall, to one's own life. It seemed to reveal one's own best ways of connecting with one's body, mind, and spirit, and through those, to develop similar connections with clients and teach them to develop connections with themselves. Following the teaching of Erickson, I saw hypnosis not as a set of techniques, but rather as a way of being, learning, teaching, and relating.

Much to my dislike, the sensational part of hypnosis was so emphasized that the most precious part—its powerful way of developing the web of deep human relationships—often remained hidden, as a precious fruit in a tropical forest. I often wondered what it would be like if more people knew about the potential of hypnosis and were able to utilize it on a daily basis. In my work with patients suffering from chronic illness and pervasive symptoms, I used hypnosis to help them develop new connections with their sensations, while at the same time teaching them to acquire specific techniques to deal with pain, fears, or anxieties.

When I became pregnant, the most natural choice was to approach pregnancy and birth through a hypnotic lens. I knew that by continuing to develop a relationship with myself, I was building connections with my developing baby. Hypnobirthing was a logical conclusion or rather, the beginning of a new relationship and a means to welcome my baby into the world in my own way. After going through the experience of a hypnobirth in a medical environment, I realized how much of my hypnosis-related experience had been made possible and sometimes facilitated by the sensitive and knowledgeable medical providers I encountered during my pregnancy. I also realized that many healthcare providers, as well as many of my friends and other expecting women, do not know about the possibilities of hypnosis-assisted birth.

Thus, this book was born out of a desire to educate providers about the extraordinary potential of hypnosis. Geared toward the gatekeepers in our medical community and people who work with pregnant women and their families, the book is a powerful tool that explains the how's and why's of hypnosis in simple, but not simplified, language. I hope that you not only enjoy and learn from this book, but also take the time to offer any comments and suggestions on how to improve it. My goal is that it can provide the most helpful information to all parties involved: future mothers, their loved ones, and the medical professionals who accompany them through their journey toward a new family.

Acknowledgments

Isaac Newton is known for saying, "If I have seen further than others, it is by standing upon the shoulders of giants." I am forever grateful to many people for making this book possible. Therefore, I would like to express my sincere gratitude to:

Dr. Milton Erickson, posthumously, for his continuous inspiration and the wisdom and knowledge that he conveyed while treating his patients with indescribable kindness. His ability to relate to his patients, seeing uniqueness in each individual, has touched my heart forever and influenced my own training and aspirations.

Dr. Douglas Flemons, for his introduction to the Ericksonian hypnosis and the training in hypnotherapy that gave me the ability to look at human relationships through a hypnotic lens, seeing how connections and disconnections can be complementary and useful in their own way.

Bill O'Hanlon, for his introduction to hypnosis and to professional writing that made me believe in myself and envision myself as a writer. While his books illustrate how to convey complex materials in an interesting and inspiring way, he made me believe that what we think and strongly believe in might be important to communicate, as it might be helpful to many people and change the lives of our future patients and clients.

Dr. Jeffrey Zeig, for his introduction to improvisational therapy and his reflections on the self of the therapist. His ability to see the therapist as a whole person rather than a technician who masters a set of techniques inspired me to seek a deeper understanding of my clients and myself.

Marie Mongan, for her introduction to HypnoBirthing, which showed me how to experience childbirth in a unique, meaningful way, as well as for her inspiration to continue exploring the influence of hypnosis on pregnancy and birthing.

Amy King and Alison Pavan, my editors at Rowman and Littlefield. Amy sought my attention and believed in this book since its conception. Her thoughtful guidance made my journey as a novice writer easier. Alison went beyond duty in her prompt responses and her support in finalizing the book for publication.

My special thank you goes to my writing editor and coach, Cindy Barrilleaux, whose special talent made this book clearer. Her dedication and continuous encouragements made me work harder to define and redefine my thoughts in order to make the material more engaging and relevant to my readers. She gave the warm critique that I needed to complete the book.

This book would not be possible without my own experience with hypnobirthing. I would like to thank my wonderful team of healthcare providers who allowed me to have the birthing that I dreamed of: my OBGYN Dr. Emmanuella Wolloch, my obstetrician Dr. Franz Rivera, my doula Diana Zacharine, and all the nurses and nursing assistants at Mount Sinai Medical Center in Miami Beach, FL.

I am also forever grateful to my husband, Thierry Watters, for his continuous support of my artistic and research endeavors; to my parents, Elvira and Nikolai Beskadarov, for their unceasing cheerleading; and to my grandmother, Lydia Lipenkova, for her continuous prayers for me.

Introduction

How can hypnosis be utilized to achieve a comfortable pregnancy and a successful birth? What information is necessary for healthcare practitioners to know in order to guide their patients who are exploring the option of a hypnobirth or considering utilizing some hypnosis-based technique during pregnancy and delivery? What are the myths about hypnosis and what would be helpful to know about hypnotic interventions to patients and their caregivers? By outlining the history of hypnosis and natural childbirth, addressing specific theoretical frameworks and clinical applications related to hypnosis, and describing specific techniques that can be practiced during pregnancy and at the time of delivery, this book guides you, the healthcare provider, in your exploration of how hypnosis can become an important part of your patients' successful birthing process.

ABOUT THIS BOOK

An abundance of books address what women can expect while pregnant and giving birth, how they can plan and accomplish a natural birth, and how they can use the diverse hypnosis-based techniques while giving birth. What makes this book different and what is the most beneficial way to use this book?

First, this book is written for caregivers of expectant women, whether mental health providers or medical health providers. It has three objectives: (1) to introduce the possibilities of hypnosis to caregivers who may be unaware of them or skeptical about them; (2) to explain how hypnosis can be useful during natural and medically supported types of birthing; and (3) to describe to providers what the pregnant woman and her support team need to do in order to benefit from hypnosis.

Being a licensed family therapist and trained to work in medical settings, I have often witnessed a disconnect between the worlds of traditional and alternative medicine. While traditionally trained practitioners may be suspicious about the proven efficacy of alternative medicine, clinicians from the alternative-medicine approach may focus on the limitations of traditional medical interventions. Each side claims their advantages and underscores the limitations of the other side.

As a systems thinker, I often have found this two-worlds approach limiting and unsupportive of patients' and clients' needs. I believe that success lies in creating the possibility to collaborate and create a hybrid approach in which each model complements the other, creating multiple opportunities for patients and their families. Writing this book is an opportunity for me to introduce medical practitioners (physicians-obstetricians, nurses, and other providers) to the possibilities of hypnosis in childbirth and beyond.

Second, I hope to demystify the myths about hypnosis as part of proving it to be a viable option for mothers facing either a natural delivery or an emergency C-section. Talking to my friends who had to change their plans while giving birth, I often felt their disappointment that their labor had to be induced or that they needed a C-section after many hours of labor. While neither future mothers nor caregivers can predict what will happen when the woman actually is giving birth, practicing hypnosis can prepare women to face the unexpected and move with the flow while trusting their bodies and their support team.

Finally, this book provides specific steps to be taken by an expecting mother and her care team in order to benefit from hypnotic interventions. While I recommend viewing hypnosis as being a philosophy of treatment more than a set of techniques, I realize that caregivers and future mothers need guidance and techniques in order to embark on this exciting adventure. To benefit from trance and its accompanying effects, the patient/client needs to develop a sense of trust not only in the world surrounding her, but most of all in her own ability to trust that world. This often starts with developing trust in her own body and mind, in her unique ability to create pathways to change, and her flexibility and wisdom. This is not done in one day. This book is an invitation and guide for providers to assist future mothers to explore the connections between the body, the mind, and the world around us. My hope for readers is that their reflections about this connection will continue beyond this book and will lead to further explorations and insights.

What is the most beneficial way to use this book? The book offers a linear progression of chapters and information. However, I invite you to use the book in the way that is most convenient for you and best meets your needs.

I hope you enjoy reading this book as much as I have enjoyed writing it. I also hope that it sparks additional conversations and new ways of relating to your clients/patients in your area of work. Most of all, I welcome any response to this book, because I perceive the subject of hypnosis in birthing as on ongoing conversation in which we can learn from one another. Your feedback is welcome!

ABOUT HYPNOSIS

When I tell people that I practice hypnosis, their usual reaction is a mix of surprise, disbelief, and curiosity. They usually ask me to describe exactly what I do when practicing hypnotic interventions with my clients. No matter what I share about my work, they ask such questions as, "Does it work?" "Can you be manipulated under hypnosis?" or "Can you get 'stuck' in trance?" Even more incredulity and questions follow when I say that I gave birth using hypnotic interventions. People have asked why I would do that to myself and how I was able to cope with the pain. I was put in the category of people who do not trust modern medical science.

In this book I address these and many other questions regarding hypnosis and hypnobirthing, starting by dismantling the many myths that surround trance and hypnosis. Most importantly I introduce and support the fact that more than a set of specific techniques, hypnosis rests on a specific state of mind, a philosophical construct, and a particular approach to life experiences. In other words, I see hypnosis not as a set of interventions, but rather as an encompassing way of being, in which we embrace, celebrate, and practice interconnectedness between our body and our mind, between our problems and their solutions, and between healers and those healed.

Not all people and researchers see hypnosis this way. In fact, there is no one specific definition of the word but rather, multiple conceptualizations of this phenomenon. Most definitions of hypnosis merely described the behavior of the "hypnotized person." Investigation of the word's etymology reveals that hypnosis "derives from the Greek word 'hypnos,' which translates into English as 'sleep'" (Rajasekaran, Edmonds, and Higginson 2005, 418). However, as Curtis (2001) emphasizes, "under hypnosis . . . patients are neither awake nor asleep, but are receptive to therapeutic suggestions to encourage a change in behavior" (604). Milton Erickson (1959) provides another definition of hypnosis as "a state of intensified attention and receptiveness and an increased responsiveness to an idea or to a set of ideas" (67).

Another important debate related to the definition of hypnosis concerns state vs. non-state theories: Is hypnosis a state of mind that we can induce in a person, or is it something else (for example, a phenomenological experience prompted by a specific context or relationship [O'Hanlon 1992])? It is important to mention this debate, because many people believe that they belong to a category of patients who cannot be hypnotized. However, this belief cannot be maintained if we understand hypnosis as a special relationship that a person chooses to experience rather than a particular state of mind that a person has to engage in against his will. (Note that in this book, the male and female pronouns will be used interchangeably unless referring to a specific gender.)

While Erickson taught the existence of a state of trance, other hypno-therapists view hypnosis as, in the words of Barber, "a social psychological phenomenon . . . as a way of interacting" (Barber, as cited in O'Hanlon and Martin 1992, 52). A third category of practitioners and researchers, such as Bill O'Hanlon for example, agree with both sides, conceptualizing hypnosis as "a distinguished state in language" (20), in which hypnotic trance is created and recreated in the process of a conversation. Finally, Flemons (2004) conceptualizes hypnosis as "the creation and mainte-nance of a special relationship" (xvi), "between people, but also between people and various parts of their experience" (50).

While multiple definitions of hypnosis have been offered (APA 2005, as cited in Bioy and Wood 2006; Douglas 1999; Yapko 1995), I am particu-larly attracted by this relational conceptualization, supported by Flemons (1999), who also described hypnosis as an experience that connects "the mindfulness of your body and the embodiment of your mind" (139). Under hypnotic trance, the boundaries that separate our physical and emotional sensations become irrelevant, thus allowing our body to learn from our mind and our mind to learn from our body. This conceptualiza-tion supports the notion that our emotional experiences influence our physical sensations, and takes this idea even further by establishing that by different connections we can achieve different understanding and ulti-mately different experiences of our physical and emotional being. This is critical to keep in mind, as many professionals involved in the birthing process have emphasized the importance of remembering that mental attitude and emotions play a crucial role in the birthing outcome (Gaskin 2003; Mongan 2005). From this perspective, hypnosis can be seen as a tool that allows future mothers to explore and get in touch with the intercon-nections between their physical state and their emotions, which, as a result, gives them the possibility to change their experiences of their body and their mind during pregnancy and while giving birth.

This relational conceptualization of hypnosis leads us to consider one of its therapeutic applications, in which "the problem can be accepted, transformed, and/or left behind" (O'Hanlon and Martin 1992, 50). Note that the goal is not to get rid of the problem, but rather to modify the future mother's and her caregivers' relationship to it. For instance, the common perception of the birthing process is as a painful experience. Viewed as such, the ultimate goal of a future mother and her healthcare practitioners becomes trying to eliminate pain or at least to minimize it. Without questioning all the reported pain associated with labor, I am often surprised not by some people's willingness to accept that pain will be part of their birthing process, but the acceptance the pain before even experiencing it. An analogy is that some people do experience nausea while travelling by boat; however, others do not. For the most part, tak-ing a cruise is not automatically associated with seasickness. Therefore, it is curious to me how we arrived at a point that pain has become so associated with birth that most people cannot imagine one without the other. In fact, a successful birth is often associated with a pain-free birth, which has become the ultimate goal for medical and alternative interventions.

Instead of starting out by seeking to minimize pain for the patient, practitioners might first explore what sensations the patient is actually experiencing. If the patient reports having pain, a hypnotherapist becomes curious about the exact sensations associated with the pain, the patient's previous experience with pain, and even the role of pain in the birthing process in different cultures. Thus, hypnosis expands our understanding of the problem rather than delineating it within a specific definition. This embraces the permissive use of language, where "might" is welcome and encouraged. By engaging in hypnosis, providers become curious about the different sensations experienced by a person without assuming that a particular sensation is taking place. In fact, hypnosis invites us to explore multiple sensations that might be described by very few words in our culture. After all, when we say "pain," do we actually know what that word encompasses for any particular person? Even when we ask someone, "What is your pain level on a scale from 1 to 10?" do we follow up to find out what 1 or 10 means for that particular person? Also, how often do we explore what it means for *us* to experience pain on a scale from 1 to 10?

Therefore, the relational understanding of hypnosis promotes taking into consideration patients' and families' needs, as well as inviting the patient to be an active participant in the plan of care. It promotes collaboration. This brings us to the third connection addressed earlier, the connection between the patient and the healthcare practitioner. To practice hypnosis, it is imperative to establish a "relationship of mutual responsiveness" (Gilligan, as cited in Yapko 1995, 16), in which the phenomenon "is controlled by the client, who can initiate or terminate the experience any time he or she chooses" (Kirsh, Lynn, and Rhue, as cited in Yapko 1995, 19). To promote and encourage such a relationship, practitioners need to explore the person's vision of the problem and solution. It invites practitioners to become curious about the person's definitions, sensations, and experiences. Ultimately, it promotes a stance of humble and respectful curiosity in which interventions are practiced *with* the person, not *for* or *to* the person, and in which each interaction is taken as an additional opportunity to learn about the person and oneself.

ABOUT BIRTH

Many books and articles have been written on the subject of birth. My intent in this book is not to compete with detailed accounts of the biological aspects of birthing, nor to give an overview of different cultural traditions surrounding it. Rather, I invite you to reflect on what the word "birth" represents to you and what it might represent to your patients and clients.

To start, think about the word "birth" and note the first three associations that come to mind. They might come in the form of a picture, word, action, melody, color, or something else. When you've noted them, next think about the influences that led to those associations. Where do you think they came from? Do you have a person or place in mind with these associations? What emotions do you experience with these associations?

The associations that came to you regarding the word "birth" represent a small part of your biological, cultural, social, and spiritual beliefs about the process of birthing. They also represent the biological, cultural, social, and spiritual influences that you have encountered in your life so far. Since all of us have different backgrounds and belief systems, we all have somewhat different representations of birth. However, if we examine them closer, we might find some common themes that unite them.

For example, when I think about birth, an image of an opening flower comes to mind; I see an image of a hospital, and I feel a strange sensation in my body, almost like a tension in my back. The opening flower reminds me of a visualization technique that I used when I gave birth to my child. The image of a hospital is an old memory of visiting my mother when she gave birth to my brother. I was not allowed to go in, but had to stay outside and wave to her as she was standing with my brother in her arms at the hospital's window. Finally, because my body remembers the sensations that I experienced when I was giving birth, when I think about it now, I can almost feel it in my bones and muscles, almost like when you remember a familiar perfume even when it is not nearby.

My experiences could be seen within the thematic frameworks of visualization, medical system, and bodily sensation. They might be similar to other people's perceptions of birth (for example, a lot of people might think about hospitals when they think about giving birth). However, if you explore the images, my experiences and sensations are quite different from those of another person who thinks about a hospital when associating with the birthing process.

This exercise illustrates two important aspects to remember while exploring hypnosis to assist during the birthing process. First, it is vital to recognize the variability of people's perceptions and experiences around the birthing process, necessitating the care provider to become curious and explore these perceptions to provide the most individualized and personalized approach for each person involved in the birthing process. Second, we, as care providers, have to engage in our own exploration of our perceptions of the birthing process as well. Since we will be involved in the process along with our clients/patients, our perceptions, beliefs, and ideas will guide and influence the perceptions, ideas, and ultimately experiences of our patients/clients. By becoming aware of our own perceptions, we become aware of the influence we might bring to the lives of people around us.

These aspects also remind us to consider the fact that different people will view a "successful" birth differently. I see care providers' task as an opportunity to discover what a successful birth looks like to each patient/client and then to help the person to contribute to that experience.

Please note that I am intentionally using the word "birth," not "labor" or "delivery." Why? Expanding on the previous exercise, think again of the associations—words, images, and sensations—that come to mind when you think about the word "birth." Now do the same exercise with the words "labor" and "delivery." Note the differences in associations. Personally, when I think about the word "labor," the only association that comes to mind is hard work without joy or satisfaction associated with it. That association is one sided, because while the birthing process can be laborious, it is definitely accompanied by joy and is celebrated in many cultures. When I think about the word "delivery," the only image that comes to mind is pizza delivery. Your associations might be completely different from mine. Ultimately, there are no bad or good images per se. What is important is to realize what influences particular words and images have on us and on the people in our care.

While some might see the above exercise as simply word musing, it is important to note that language is one of the unique ways we have to explore and understand the worlds of others. While we are somewhat constrained by our own language categories (what German philosopher Ludwig Wittgenstein called "being bewitched by our own language"), with willingness and curiosity we can have a glimpse in another person's mind.

The mind is an important construct that will be addressed often in this book. Since hypnosis involves a particular connection between our body and our mind, it is vital to understand how this connection can help during the birthing process. Based on certain research studies (Conkling 2002; England and Horowitz 1998; Gaskin 2003), in this book we will assume that birthing process cannot be seen just as a physiological process (for example, the opening of a cervix so the baby can get through). While it is important to know and understand the biological aspect of birthing, it is as important to understand the psychosocial aspect of the birthing process, such as the influence of emotions on the progression of the biological process and the influence of social traditions on the biological aspect of birthing. Finally, it is also important to consider the influence of the spiritual beliefs of the mother and her family on the birthing process. After all, the door to other people's worlds can only be open when we listen intently with our body, mind, and heart. It will be important to take time to listen to and ask questions of the expecting mothers, as it will allow you to establish connections with your patients, which ultimately will lead to a more satisfying birth for all parties involved.

WHY'S AND HOW'S OF HYPNOSIS

One of my goals in writing this book was to explain the why's and how's of hypnosis. The why's refer to the theoretical foundations of hypnosis, its historical development, and specific applications. The how's refer directly to the context of childbirth and specific techniques that can prepare the expectant mother to use hypnosis during pregnancy and birthing. The first part of the book contains an historical overview of hypnosis and the childbirth movement. I trace the development and application of hypnosis from its earliest days to today, highlighting major shifts in theoretical frameworks over the decades. The second part of the book provides specific examples and stories of the optimal use of hypnosis and how it can expand the expectant mother's thinking and attitudes as well as positively influence the conversation between the medical provider and the patient before and during delivery.

In order to help the expectant mother make informed choices regarding hypnosis, it is essential to have a firm grounding in the meaning of hypnosis so you can explore with her what it has to offer. Chapter 1 provides theoretical definitions and a brief history of hypnosis, dismantling various myths and defining the theoretical underpinnings of the hypnotic approach that I believe is most helpful during labor. In chapter 2, I discuss the context of the natural birth as well as the hypnobirth movement. While the philosophical foundations of these approaches to birth overlap, there are also distinct differences. This chapter also clarifies the difference between the hypnobirth movement and the broader possibilities of hypnosis beyond that specific approach to birthing. Chapter 3 provides theoretical support for and reflections on the interconnections of our physical, emotional, and spiritual experiences and ways they feed one another. This chapter suggests a larger context for the use of hypnosis, in the framework of a unique approach not only toward healthcare, but also toward the experience of life in general. This leads to reflections on the strong connections that can be established between the baby and the mother by using hypnosis during the childbirth.

Chapter 4 begins the second part of the book, with a noticeable shift in the focus. Here I address the preparations for the childbirth, which begin long before the actual day, from the perspective of the use of hypnosis during labor. I describe the importance of and techniques for creating a unique vision for delivery and building a supportive team that will help her to fulfill that vision by using the philosophy of hypnosis during the childbirth. The reader will discover the distinction between the overall approach of hypnobirth and specific hypnotic techniques that the provider can help the woman use before and during labor.

This chapter also explores how the philosophy of hypnosis, with its focus on the present moment and interconnections, deepens the experience of childbirth. This is important to its use in hypnobirth and facilitates experiencing life while being mindful of the interrelationships between everything and everyone. When understood in this broad context of meaningful connections and unique opportunities, hypnosis can open the woman's eyes and heart to exceptional experiences. This viewpoint avoids the problem of techniques learned and practiced in isolation, on which the woman relies to guarantee her particular expectation of the birthing experience. Instead, this understanding of hypnosis creates an atmosphere of curiosity and openness rather than setting the stage for a performance accompanied by specific acts.

Moving forward, chapter 5 shifts further from the theoretical overview of hypnosis to address its practical applications, including specific techniques in preparation for and during labor. This chapter sets the stage for the practical, or "how to," focus by exploring the role of imagery and breathing in hypnotic induction. Chapter 6 introduces the benefits of using music, yoga, and visualization in hypnobirth.

The book then moves forward to discuss hypnobirth in action (chapter 7). One of the questions that I often hear is "Does hypnosis really work while you are in labor?" In this chapter, I address several points for healthcare providers to remember during the birthing process, such as the importance of the language used to create the optimal environment for the hypnotic interventions. I also review techniques that are helpful specifically in the moment of giving birth. Chapter 8 complements chapter 7 by providing specific techniques for symptom management and medically assisted birth.

Finally, chapter 9 brings to light the life that welcomes both the mother and the baby after the birth. These encompass the highest possibilities of hypnosis, which arise naturally from its approach to any life experience. Once hypnosis has been accepted as a life stance, opening one's heart to experiment and curiosity, it provides endless opportunities for greater awareness of interconnections. So in truth, my goal for this book is not only to provide any particular applications of hypnosis to birthing, but also to invite you, the provider, and through you the expectant mother, to reconsider the implications of your relationships and their constructions or absence in your life experience and that of those around you. Thus, the invitation to explore hypnosis is also an invitation to explore the possibilities brought by hypnosis for a deeper, broader life.

In addition to the described chapters, I included several documents that might serve as a helpful reminder of various techniques covered in this book (Appendix A), various terms that I use in this text (Glossary), and fundamental theoretical ideas pertaining to hypnosis (Appendix B). These documents serve as a quick go-to place to review specific material from a chapter of the book or to check an unfamiliar term.

ONE

Introduction to Hypnosis

The nature of hypnosis is complex, and the study of different hypnotic elements is still in process today. Most of what is known about hypnosis is based on the examinations of its applications and our experiences of the phenomenon. To address applications of hypnosis in preparation for and during the childbirth, one first needs to come to agreement on what hypnosis is. To achieve this understanding, this chapter reviews the history of hypnosis, dismantles common myths of hypnosis, and clarifies frequent questions that I often hear about the practice of hypnosis.

A HISTORY OF HYPNOSIS

To present the history of hypnosis, one first needs to understand what hypnosis is. The word itself provokes mixed reactions and articulating a specific definition of the phenomenon turns out to be a challenge. In fact, the understanding of hypnosis has been changing from the eighteenth to the twenty-first century as new theoretical and philosophical paradigms have been adopted, providing new ways to articulate additional explanations (Vandenberg 2010).

The first documented use of hypnosis is attributed to a Viennese physician, Franz Anton Messmer, and an Austrian priest, Johann Joseph Gassner (Green, Laurence, and Lynn 2014; Peter 2005; Vandenberg 2010). Messmer and Gassner disputed the role of this first precursor of modern hypnosis, and their disagreement expanded into a large debate. In the eighteenth century, Messmer developed his theory of animal magnetism, in which hypnotists used magnets to change patients' physical and mental conditions. While Messmer promoted the use of hypnosis-related techniques based on neurophysiological treatment, his opponent, Gassner, practiced as an exorcist healer, with interventions based on his spiritual understanding of the development of illness. It is interesting to note that Messmer was more successful in promoting his approach—one of the first victories of the scientific approach to treatment over a religious approach toward healing.

In the early history of hypnosis, most attention was paid to the influence of the hypnotist and his role in the successful outcome of the healing process. As an illustration, in 1784, Benjamin Franklin investigated Messmer's theory of animal magnetism, which paid particular attention to both the relationship between the patient and the hypnotist and his powerful influence on his subjects.

Based on the theory of animal magnetism, two additional healing approaches were developed: mediumship and spiritualism. The first explored the role of unconscious forces within the individual, and the second advanced a theory of multiple personalities (Green et al. 2014). Thus, an interest in exploring hypnotic influence led to the later development of psychological and psychotherapeutic theories. As Vandenberg (2010) emphasizes, "hypnosis is one of the most provocatively generative topics in the history of psychology, giving rise to psychotherapy, personality theories, formulations of unconscious processes, and appreciation of the power of suggestion and social influence" (51).

Another indisputable relationship lies between hypnosis and medical science (Bioy 2006). In fact, in the nineteenth century the evolution of hypnosis was closely related to its medical utilization. With the discovery of such phenomena as analgesia, anamnesis, and time regression, hypnosis was implemented and documented in many clinical case studies. For example, Scottish physician James Esdaile was known to use hypnosis as an analgesic during major surgical procedures (Conkling 2002).

While the eighteenth century had been marked by the exploration of the hypnotist's traits, the nineteenth century was noted for its examination of the role of suggestibility during hypnotic intervention. One of the most influential figures in the hypnosis movement of that time, noted by many as the father of modern hypnosis, was the Scottish surgeon James Braid. With the publication of *Neurypnology* (1843), Braid coined the term "hypnosis" (Conkling 2002). While the concept of suggestibility had been considered before Braid (Green et al. 2014), he deepened the understanding of hypnosis by further exploring the role of hypnotic suggestion rather than simply focusing attention on the phenomenon of hypnotic trance. Now the attention was refocused from the role of the hypnotist to the traits of subjects (Lynn and Rhue 1991).

In the early twentieth century, French psychologist Pierre Janet articulated new psychological theories, coining such terms as "subconscious," "dissociation," and "automatism." In line with this new development, the role of induction diminished while the importance of suggestion was expanded (Green et al. 2014). With these additional psychological concepts, as well as the famous work of French physician Hippolyte Bernheim (1840–1919), the explanation of the hypnotic phenomenon shifted even further from external causes to psychological causes. This psychological theoretical framework replaced the biomedical understanding of the pioneers of the hypnotic movement and became the accepted model of reference moving forward (Vandenberg 2010).

The development of hypnosis in the beginning of the twentieth century was marked by the birth of experimental psychology. The hypothesis of suggestibility was still being explored, but the focus was placed on the researcher's ability to support his argument by conducting a controlled experiment and producing supporting quantitative data. The collection of individual cases demonstrating a successful outcome was no longer sufficient.

The work of American psychologist Clark Hull provides the perfect example of how the hypnotic phenomenon was studied with the precision of exact science. Hull's fundamental work, *Hypnosis and Suggestibility* (1933), influenced the field of hypnosis and changed the discussion by putting the phenomenon in the framework of behavioral theory. Based on his experiments, Hull found that the only difference between people experiencing hypnosis and the control subjects was an increased susceptibility to suggestions, the cause of which Hull explained as increased muscle relaxation and induction. Thus, the study of hypnosis was reduced to a quantitative difference in susceptibility. This led to a major shift in the understanding of hypnosis in terms of acquired response to stimuli, such as sounds, rather than a response associated with specific ideas. This conceptualization is a perfect example of a positivist framework of understanding of a specific phenomenon (Vandenberg 2010).

Another major influence in the exploration of hypnosis was WWII and the subsequent sense of urgency to prepare efficient soldiers and to heal traumatized and wounded veterans. Efforts to produce effective treatments became centralized and organized. For example, the Society for Clinical and Experimental Hypnosis was founded in 1950. In 1955, the British Medical Association approved hypnotherapy as a valid medical treatment. The American Society of Clinical Hypnosis was founded in 1958, and board certification for practitioners of hypnosis was credentialed in 1960. A division of APA for the study of hypnosis was created in 1969. By this time, the study of hypnosis was legitimized and validated by academic circles.

The late twentieth century brought a new understanding of the hypnotic phenomenon. In 1962, the publication of *Structure of Scientific Revolution*, by American physicist Thomas Kuhn, challenged the work and philosophical paradigm of Clark Hull and other hypnosis researchers operating within a positivist framework. Kuhn introduced a nonlinear approach to the study of life and science and the introduction of the word "paradigm" in the scientific realm opened a door for the development of such philosophical movements as constructivism and post-modernism.

These scientific developments influenced the conceptualization of hypnosis, bringing a broader understanding of the relational connections involved in the creation and experience of a trance-like phenomenon.

In line with the described positivist framework, the understandings and conceptualizations of hypnosis were also influenced by the development of psychological testing and the concept of construct validity proposed in the 1960s by American educational psychologist Lee Chronback and psychologist Paul Meehl. Differentiating between the concepts of intervening variable and hypothetical construct, these theoreticians claimed that inference from data to theory could be theoretically defensible. Thus, the concept of the construct itself presupposed that the description of a phenomenon was accepted to be the most viable, without presupposing that it completely reflects a reality (Vandenberg 2010). In line with this discovery, the exact conceptualization of hypnosis was less relevant: the interest became focused on its effects and benefits.

Following these shifts in paradigm, further explanations of hypnosis were developed. One of the important theories that polarized theoreticians and practitioners of hypnosis was the neodissociative model of hypnosis, advocated by American psychologist Ernest Hilgard. Hilgard stated that the explanation of hypnosis does not rely on observable behaviors (as defended earlier by Hull), but relies on the intra-psychic structures of individuals, which can be inferred from their responsivity. Following this idea, in 1959 Hilgard developed the now famous Hypnotic Susceptibility Scale, based on the idea that the hypnotizability has state-like traits. From this perspective, the more receptive the person to a specific suggestion given during the research procedure, the more susceptible this individual will be to a hypnotic induction. The scale, somewhat modified, is still in use today.

Hilgard also conceptualized hypnosis as a state that induces a special disjuncture of presumed cognitive hierarchy. This means that different levels of cognition can be activated by hypnotic suggestion, directly bypassing the usual executive control system (Lynn and Rhue 1991). In essence, "not all action is consciously intended, initiated, or controlled" (Lynn and Rhue, 6). By establishing a new responsive system, an individual under hypnosis may experience alternative sensations and behaviors to what would be expected in a particular situation (for example, a person might experience surprise rather than suffering in response to a painful stimulus).

Opposing Hilgard's approach described above, a neobehavioral model proposed by Theodor Barber (1960) and Nicholas Spanos (1990) promoted a non-state understanding of hypnosis. Both researchers claimed that the phenomenon could be explained by social-situational factors in which subjects experience hypnosis as a result of contextual influence, cognitive interpretations of the people under hypnosis by a hypnotist, and the influence of social expectations. In this conceptualization, both hypnotist and subject evoke a hypnotic experience based on a shared common cultural knowledge about hypnosis (Vandenberg 2010).

While the state versus non-state debate can be considered ongoing, some researchers have pointed out the necessity for new, more current conceptualizations of the hypnotic phenomenon (Vandenberg 2010). Taking into consideration the biopsychosocial framework articulated by George Engel in the 1970s, in which mind and body are interconnected and psychology and medicine are brought together for more individualized care of patients and their families, one is left wondering what the best framework is for understanding hypnosis.

One of the conceptualizations offered in this book views hypnosis in terms of relationship. This theory, from Canadian family therapist Douglas Flemons (2001), promotes an understanding of hypnosis as a unique connection between body and mind facilitated by the special relationship between hypnotist and subject. In this view, rather than helping patients dissociate from their problems, the hypnotist strives to help the client *associate* with the problem, but in a new, more meaningful way. By inviting clients to experience a stronger connection between their body and their mind, the hypnotist helps them establish a new understanding of their particular challenges. This approach of Flemons was inspired by the writings of American anthropologist Gregory Bateson, who viewed the world in terms of "dynamic relationships," and brain activity in terms of a constant creation of meaningful boundaries and connections with the world around us. Paraphrasing Bateson, Flemons (2001) writes, "Where there's no difference, there's no boundary, and where there's no boundary, there's no perception" (139). Thus, hypnotic interventions may be used to assist patients to make meaningful connections and separations, possibly altering their symptoms by creating new, meaningful ways of relating to their world.

Another important influence on the relational understanding of hypnosis is the Ericksonian approach to hypnosis, which is discussed next.

ERICKSONIAN HYPNOSIS

American psychiatrist Milton Erickson, MD (1901–1980), is considered one of the most influential figures in the history of hypnosis. His unique approach represented an important paradigm shift in attitudes toward the history of hypnosis and provided the foundation for new approaches in hypnosis, hypnotherapy, and psychotherapy. A student of Clark Hull, Erickson contributed to the progress of clinical hypnosis; his work was characterized by a distinctive philosophical stance and new techniques of humanistic hypnosis and psychotherapy.

One of the most unique features of his approach derived from Erickson's belief in human strength and resilience. Erickson theorized that people already possess the solution to their problems, but are not always able to access it freely. The hypnotherapist, he taught, acts as a mediator facilitating access to knowledge between different parts of the subject's mind where knowledge and solutions reside. In this way, the hypnotist helps the patient discover their own incredible basis of know-how, leading to new ways to experience the same situation. This conceptualization of the mind is radically different from Freud's, in which most of the content of the unconscious is unacceptable, shameful, and best contained and neutralized by one's conscious mind.

Using an example from the birthing process to illustrate Erickson's approach, the hypnotist's attitude is that each woman has a specific, but perhaps hidden, representation of a successful birthing process that can be explored and reinforced by hypnosis. By establishing interconnections with the future mother's previous experiences of managing her body and emotions, the hypnotist helps an expectant mother discover and use her existing and necessary skills during her birthing process.

Erickson maintained that most of our functioning occurs unconsciously (O'Hanlon and Wilk 1987). About the value of operationalizing the unconscious, Erickson notes: "Now the unconscious mind is a vast storehouse of your memories, your learnings. It has to be a storehouse because you cannot keep consciously in mind all the things you know. Considering all the learnings you acquired in the lifetime, you use the vast majority of them automatically in order to function" (Zeig 1980, 175). This storing of learnings is understood to be the most efficient way of organizing our experiences. In addition, the Ericksonian approach assumed that patterns of organization (such as emotional patterns) are not necessarily linear but operate according to their own logic. To change the pattern, the hypnotist adopts this nonlinear communication, so that hypnosis can engender therapeutic communication between different parts of the client's mind. Thus, hypnosis can be viewed as "a form of injunctive communication in which the patient starts to respond to the underlying meaning, to the connotation in the communication" (Zeig 2006, 55).

Another important aspect of Ericksonian hypnosis is its personalized and flexible approach to understanding human problems and to implementing specific solutions. In fact, this flexibility, or "the readiness of the therapist to respond strategically to any and all aspects of the patients or the environment" (Zeig 2006, xx), became known as "utilization" and was recognized as the cornerstone of the Ericksonian approach (Green et al. 2014). The hypnotist practicing from this perspective becomes curious about the patient's unique characteristics and instead of trying to dissolve or ignore them, uses them to design individualized hypnotic interventions. Erickson addressed that important feature of his approach by stating that "each person is a unique individual; hence therapy should be formulated to meet the uniqueness of the individual's needs, rather than tailoring the person to fit the procrustean bed of a hypothetical theory of human behavior" (Zeig 2006, 13).

It is fair to state that utilization provided the framework for the application of this model, by which the hypnotist aims to do the following:

- Elicit the patient's resources: the approach is future-oriented and promotes a hopeful view of the patient's and therapist's abilities to reach a desirable outcome.
- Tailor hypnotic interventions: the Ericksonian approach is patient-centered at every step (for example, induction, deepening, or termination). In comparison to more traditional and linear hypnosis, this approach surprises by its flexibility. Not only is the hypnotist not required to follow a specific order proceeding from induction to termination, but also each stage is initiated with interventions specifically designed for the subject. In traditional hypnosis, the hypnotist starts by ascertaining the patient's hypnotic capacity, uses a predesigned script, intensifies the subject's experience with a direct suggestion, offers direct suggestion to address the problem, and then reorients the patient. In Ericksonian hypnosis, each subject is seen as capable of experiencing hypnosis; the script is almost non-existent because each intervention is designed to fit a specific person's needs; the suggestions are offered in a permissive form (for example, the word "might" is often used to allow the subject an opportunity to adjust the induction to his or her own experience of the hypnotic process). Erickson did not believe that formal induction was needed to support subjects' responsiveness (Zeig 2006).
- Acknowledges the power of context: to change a particular pattern, the hypnotist aims to transform the context of that pattern. Such change may be introduced in three distinctive ways: decontextualization, recontextualization, and reframing. In decontextualization, the hypnotist's aim is to abolish a particular current context. As Gregory Bateson (2000) noted, information is the difference in context that makes a difference. Therefore, either the difference or the perception of the difference is obscured for the observer (O'Hanlon and Wilk 1987). For example, rather than seeing a hospital as a medical establishment with all the attributes of such, an expectant mother can chose to ignore its medical attributes (for example, OR, catheter, and so on) and choose to see it as a birthing center. Recontextualization offers an opportunity to introduce new context markers through new behaviors, perceptions, or objects. Inviting a doula to be present during a birthing process in a hospital recontextualizes the environment by adding the attribute of a birthing center. By reframing, the hypnotist helps the client transfer contextual know-how to a different context (O'Hanlon and Wilk). For example, if a woman first gave birth in a birthing center but for the

second birth has to have an emergency C-section in a hospital, the hypnotist can reframe the situation by pointing out that her body was smart enough to ask for help in order to provide a safe birthing experience to the mother and her child.

- Promotes states of responsiveness: the hypnotist responds to the subject's smallest cues, including the client's facial expressions, in order to design individualized inductions and suggestions. The therapist trains his perceptions to notice the subject's manifestations in the hypnotic process and to use them in the process of induction. For example, the hypnotist notes and utilizes such details as the patient's breathing, blinking, or sweating. On the other hand, the patient also assumes a posture of responsiveness to subtle cues from the therapist. Therefore, in interactive terms, hypnosis can be defined as "the response readiness of the patient as a function of the response readiness of the therapist" (Zeig 2006, 71).
- Uses words strategically and consciously: Erickson was known for his surgical precision with words. He used each sentence to elicit a specific response or hypnotic experience. He communicated with intentionality and clients responded to the specific, subtle nuances of his communication (Zeig 2006).
- Adopts an experiential learning model: rather than viewing hypnosis as a clinician's ability to provide the patient with a specific answer to a problem via a direct suggestion, an Ericksonian therapist views his goal as the "reawakening of patient's dormant resources" (Zeig 2006, 58). The learning is viewed as intuitive rather than cognitive. While describing this feature of the Ericksonian approach, Zeig uses the term "guided association," by which the hypnotist aims to change the patient's behavior, feelings, cognition, or attitude by changing the stream of preconscious associations and invoking the re-association of the patient's internal life. Rather than providing clients with a specific direction toward problem resolution, the hypnotist orients the subject toward possible paths of success without necessarily providing a complete resolution.

It is important to note that the Ericksonian model should be conceptualized as a way of being, rather than a particular technique. To emphasize the importance of viewing this approach as a life stance, Zeig (2006) proposed to use the term "postures" rather than techniques or interventions. Therefore, what is particularly emphasized is the personal development of the hypnotist and his ability to develop and utilize his own conscious and unconscious resources. To use a metaphor, in this approach the hypnotherapist is the traveling companion sharing multiple experiences of the patient, rather than a tour guide watching those experiences from a distance (Zeig).

In describing hypnosis, Erickson was clear that he viewed hypnosis as a state. However, he refrained from providing one particular definition of hypnosis, aiming to account for multiple perspectives of several people who might be included in the hypnotic encounter. After all, the experience and the aim of hypnosis are different if we see it from the point of view of an observer, a subject, or a therapist. In addition, being reluctant to objectify the hypnotic experience and thus limit it to one theoretical lens, Erickson maintained an a-theoretical position. The description provided by Zeig (2006), "hypnosis as . . . an experiential bridge between the land of the problems and the land of solutions" (62), can serve as a broad summary of Erickson's conceptualization of hypnosis.

ERICKSON'S PUPILS

Although Milton Erickson is considered one of the most prominent figures of hypnosis in the twentieth century, it is difficult to completely account for his influence. However, several prominent practitioners have been inspired by Erickson's vision of hypnosis and incorporated it in their clinical work. These are the hypnotherapists who also inspired me to apply hypnosis in my clinical work and during my own birthing process. Ultimately they inspired me to write this book.

Bill O'Hanlon

Bill O'Hanlon is an American psychotherapist, prolific writer, and internationally known presenter on the topic of hypnosis and psychotherapy. O'Hanlon is one of only a few people who studied personally with Milton Erickson. He later developed his strength-based approach called Solution-Oriented therapy (also known as Possibility therapy). The main points of this approach are in line with Ericksonian ideas and promote the following:

- Flexibility, in which assessment, interventions, and solutions are designed with a particular client's needs in mind. Possibility therapy is based on one of the cornerstones of the Ericksonian approach, utilization. As O'Hanlon (1992) writes in *Solution-Oriented Hypnosis*, "use whatever the person is bringing into therapy" (5). He emphasizes that there is no one particular way to approach a problem; rather there are multiple ways of creating solutions to a client's problem.
- Validation, in which the client's emotions and experiences are the focus of exploration. Under the direction of a therapist, clients can learn from and utilize their past experiences. This is in line with the Ericksonian idea that the unconscious often stores useful aspects of our experience and by accessing this marvelous cave of Ali Baba,

clients can find precious resources that can transfer to their present experiences and solve their current problems. O'Hanlon views hypnosis as a possibility to "evoke the person's experience" and "transfer it across" to a situation that presents a challenge" (O'Hanlon and Martin 1992, 118).

- Precision of language, in which the therapist uses a "purposeful selection of stories" (O'Hanlon and Martin 1992, 52) to explore the client's problem and find a solution. Erickson was known for his precise use of language, as well as for his colorful, client-specific metaphors, stories, and symbols.

One aspect of O'Hanlon's conceptualization of hypnosis differs from the Ericksonian approach, but is very much in line with my understanding of hypnosis. Commenting on the ongoing debate of state versus non-state theories, O'Hanlon views hypnosis as "a distinguished state in language" (O'Hanlon and Martin 1992, 52). Adopting a social constructionist's perspective, O'Hanlon explains that rather than seeing hypnosis as "a specific thing," one can view it as an experiential phenomenon (similar to love, for example) that has been categorized as a specific experience based on repeated and shared descriptions of the phenomenon. From these accounts, a common understanding of hypnosis has been generated and continues to change as we continue to experience it and share our experiences.

I particularly value this description because it emphasizes the multiple possibilities opened by hypnosis: possibilities of inducing, experiencing, and describing hypnosis. It opens doors to further explorations and invites practitioners to embrace their creativity. It also brings out the reality that some experiences and descriptions of hypnosis remain unaccounted for and thus as yet unknown. This view of hypnosis partially applies to the utilization of hypnosis—particularly Ericksonian hypnosis—during childbirth. There are still stories to be told, discoveries to be made, and definitions to be established.

Jeffrey Zeig

Jeffrey Zeig, PhD, a well-known psychologist, marriage and family therapist, author, and presenter, also studied with Milton Erickson. He is the founder and co-director of the Milton Erickson Foundation. He taught Erickson's views of hypnosis and psychotherapy as resting on the therapist's way of being rather than way of doing. Zeig (2006) places particular emphasis on the therapist's personal development and the use of self in therapy. He expanded on Erickson's attention to individual and therapeutic flexibility, exploring how a clinician can develop and use his different ways of being, which he called "postures," in clinical work.

In line with the Ericksonian approach of utilization, Zeig (2006) also emphasizes the necessity of following the client's lead in developing and implementing client-centered solutions based on the client's abilities. To use Zeig's words, "Change does not necessarily happen because therapists communicate things that are meaningful. Often it happens because therapists communicate things meaningfully" (216). Only by proposing solutions that the client can understand and appreciate are therapists able to make changes in the client's life. To promote the change in clients' lives, Zeig also encouraged joining with clients in their own frame of reference using their own value system.

This approach is particularly helpful in exploring the use of hypnosis during the birthing process. Because each birth is essentially a unique experience, hypnotic interventions for an expecting mother should reflect the mother's definition of a successful birth, expectations of the birthing process, and unique fears and joys before and during pregnancy.

Zeig also picked up on the reach and precise language of Ericksonian hypnosis. He not only pointed out the benefits of metaphors, stories, and symbols in this approach, but also highlighted the fact that the hypnotic phenomenon was a specific communication pattern between the hypnotist and the subject. Zeig (2006) states, "One way to define trance is to call it that period in which the recipient of the communication perceives that there is more to the communication than just the detonation of words. . . . Like fine poetry, each image, each element of the communication was chosen with care for multilevel effect" (218). Thus, the particular use of language invites two people to experience a phenomenon in which words can produce change. Such careful communication becomes part of the interaction of the therapist and the client. Thus, hypnosis is viewed as an interpersonal rather than an intrapersonal phenomenon (Zeig).

Such conceptualization presents hypnosis as a collaborative process, in which both clinician and client work together to induce desired change. The client is not a passive recipient, but an active participant in his or her own experience. This is an important consideration to address when we apply it to the birthing process, in which the future mother becomes the ultimate director of her childbirth, and the clinician is a collaborator in the process.

Douglas Flemons

Douglas Flemons, PhD, a family therapist, teaches and practices Ericksonian hypnosis in academic and clinical settings. In his book, *Of One Mind*, Flemons (2001) teaches the relational understanding of hypnosis, which corresponds to the interactional view described above. In this theoretical framework, relational interconnection is essential for any changes to occur in the client's experience of a particular life situation. Relations or connections comprise multiple levels of clients' experiences.

One such connection is between our body and our mind. Consciously or unconsciously, we experience this connection or disconnection. For example, if a pregnant woman is afraid, her body tenses, preventing an optimal opening of the cervix. Besides the mind-body connection, a connection needs to be established between the client and therapist in order to produce change in the client's situation. If a client does not see a therapist as a valuable contributor to a meaningful conversation, change will not occur. Thus, a required part of a successful hypnosis is the ability to establish a meaningful relationship between the people involved in a hypnotic encounter.

Rearrangement of these connections creates new experiential possibilities. This touches again on Erickson's view of volitional rather than cognitive learning. Hypnosis offers the possibility to "experience the mindfulness of [the] body and the embodiment of [the] mind" (Flemons 2001, 139) and helps the client to experience unity between the inner and outer influences on the client's personal world and connections to external systems (for example, school system, work system, family, and so on). This is similar to the way a pianist assists the piano to produce a beautiful sound. All the notes are there, but the piano needs the vital touch of a person who knows how to play them.

To continue with the analogy of playing the piano to hypnosis, in creating music, no notes are negated or dismissed, but a new pattern is offered to arrange the notes, producing a new, harmonious melody. In the same way, Ericksonian hypnosis offers a way to alter rather than negate the client's symptoms (Flemons 2001), to change the client's relationship to the problem. It is by recontextualizing the problem, ultimately seeing it in a new light, that a hypnotherapist opens the door to possibilities. In fact, the melody was always there, the therapist is able to hear it and to help the client hear it as well.

OLD AND NEW: MYTHS ABOUT HYPNOSIS

When I tell people that I am a certified hypnotherapist and practice hypnosis with my clients, I am usually met with skepticism or humor. The conversation becomes even more interesting when I share that I implemented hypnobirth during my own labor. I distinctly remember a conversation with one physician who asked me why I would do such a thing to myself. This attitude obviously implied incredulity about the validity and effectiveness of hypnosis.

Such reactions make me consider how the media continue to shape our representations of hypnosis. Engrained in public consciousness is the image of a flamboyant person standing on a stage, using some object to induce another person into a stupor-like state. The "hypnotist" then waves a magic wand to make the subject bark like a dog, or give up significant money, or take some other undesired action. Above, I dismantled these misrepresentations by providing a history of hypnosis. I also described some hypnosis techniques and the trained hypnotist's abilities.

However, many myths remain. Below I deconstruct specific myths about hypnosis that I often hear. I also clarify again what can and what should not be expected from hypnosis, especially in the context of the childbirth. I refer to the work of a famous hypnotherapist, Dr. Michael Yapko, and his book *Essentials of Hypnosis.*

Myth 1: All Hypnosis Is the Same

There are many reasons why people would practice hypnosis. We often differentiate between experimental hypnosis (studied, for example, by Hall) and clinical hypnosis (used by such hypnotherapists as Erickson and Zeig). These different forms of hypnosis address different needs and set up different expectations in the subject of the hypnotic interaction. While sensational hypnosis is set up as entertainment, "clinical hypnosis is a system of skilled and influential communication that teaches how *words can heal* [*sic*]" (Yapko 1995, 3). Moreover, "[clinical hypnosis] minimizes the use of incarnation and rituals in its use, instead of emphasizing a rapid assessment of and sensitive responsiveness to individual client needs" (3). In addition, further distinctions can be established within different types of hypnosis. For example, clinical hypnosis can be practiced within a traditional framework or an Ericksonian approach. Also, depending on the theoretical position of a therapist, hypnotic induction and intervention may vary considerably.

Myth 2: Hypnosis Is a Last Resort Treatment

While some people remain very skeptical about hypnosis, others view it as a mysterious, somewhat dangerous, last resort treatment that can magically cure almost any disease or improve any condition. Albeit that hypnosis can be utilized in a variety of settings and for a variety of human problems, certain situations respond better to hypnosis than others. Hypnosis requires the client's active participation and the establishment of a successful working relationship between the hypnotist and the client. Hence, many subjective variables can lead to the success or failure of an intervention. In the same way that a specific therapeutic regime might work better for one patient than another (due to many variables, such as comorbidities, social support, and so on), a hypnotic intervention by a specific hypnotherapist might be more effective for some than for others.

Myth 3: A Special Environment Is Required to Induce Trance

Many people think that a perfectly structured environment is necessary for a person to be hypnotized. This idea raises the image of the client
lying down comfortably, while the therapist plays relaxing music and
uses a pendulum to induce trance.

Milton Erickson cut through this myth, by introducing the concept of
utilization. A skilled hypnotist is able to use anything in the client's environment for trance induction. In fact, having a fixed environment presup-
poses that the context works equally well for everyone, negating the
individualized-approach to the human condition promoted by the Ericksonian model.

Myth 4: The Hypnotist Controls the Client's Mind

The definitions of hypnosis (see History of Hypnosis above) as relational address this myth. Stephen Gilligan (1987) describes hypnosis as a
"relationship of mutual responsiveness" (25). The only power that a hypnotist has is to invite the client into the exploration of this new relationship called hypnosis. As Jay Haley summarized (1993), "I can only hyp-
notize you by you hypnotizing yourself: I can only help you by you
helping yourself" (15). In fact, many professionals view all hypnosis as a
self-hypnosis (Flemons 2001), while others point out that a hypnotist
needs to be experiencing hypnosis himself in order to engage to the client
in a therapeutic relationship (Zeig 2006). Thus, the experience can only be
seen as a mutual experience, where one is guiding another to take the
next step.

Myth 5: It Is Possible for the Client to Become Stuck in the Hypnotic State

This myth brings us back to the earlier discussion about the state
versus non-state theory of hypnosis. Many researchers believe that hypnosis is actually not a state, which cuts through this myth altogether. Not
only that, but even if we accept that hypnosis is a specific state with
definite attributes, hypnosis needs to be initiated by the client as much as
by the therapist. Whenever the client is no longer willing to share the
experience, the hypnotist will no longer be able to maintain the hypnosis.

Myth 6: Hypnosis Is Just a Synonym for Sleep or Relaxation

This myth may have risen because the etymology of the word "hypnosis" indicates that it "derives from the Greek word 'hypnos,' which translates into English as sleep" (Rajasekaran, Edmonds, and Higginson 2005,
418). However, Curtis (2001) stated, "Under hypnosis . . . patients are
neither awake nor asleep, but are receptive to therapeutic suggestions to
encourage a change in behavior" (604). erickson (1959) confirms that hyp-

nosis is unrelated to sleep when he points out that hypnosis is "a state of intensified attention and receptiveness and an increased responsiveness to an idea or to a set of ideas" (67).

Myth 7: Hypnosis Can Be Used for Recalling Memories

This myth rests on an inaccurate view of memory as a storage bin in which we collect our belongings with the expectation of retrieving them in perfect condition. Rather, memory should be conceptualized as a figure made of ice. Each time you bring it out, it has the potential to melt and subsequently to take on a different shape. You can also inadvertently take off a small piece of the ice figure, thus even slightly changing the whole without being aware of it. In other words, memory is not static, but changes every time we decide to have access to specific experiences and share them with others (Flemons and Wright 1999). Because accessing memories is as interactive as establishing a hypnotic relationship, hypnosis can't be used to provide a completely accurate recollection of a specific experience.

Myth 8: I Have Never Experienced Hypnosis

This statement falls in the realm of myth because most people have experienced at least some form of a mild trance, which is a form of hypnosis. Some familiar examples include watching a sports event, a theatrical play, or a movie. In each of those, the people in the audience are often so absorbed by the show and unaware of time passing that they feel as if they actually become one of the participants in the show. Another example is our ability to drive in a familiar area without noticing each turn of the road that we are on. Somehow we realize that we arrive when we see our home, but we do not remember how we got there. These are all experiences of hypnosis.

Myth 9: I Can Only Use Hypnosis as Part of a Natural Birth

This common myth is one reason I wrote this book. When I talk about hypnosis with expectant mothers, some picture a hippie-like environment that disallows any medical intervention. They often believe that hypnosis is the only way to assist in labor. While hypnotherapy has common roots with natural and hypnobirthing movements, hypnotic interventions and a hypnotic stance as described in this book can be adopted in any circumstances. In fact, hypnosis can be as beneficial during an emergency C-section as during a natural vaginal birth. Although hypnotic interventions have different purposes in the different contexts, the ultimate outcome, enhancing the well-being of the mother and baby, can be achieved in both situations.

In the twenty-first century, hypnosis is both a victim of its own success and a victim of outdated misconceptions. Unrealistic expectations have fed fear and skepticism. To avoid these myths, it is important to provide at least minimal education to future mothers early in their pregnancy, as well as to the expectant mother, who is considering using hypnosis during birth.

FREQUENTLY ASKED QUESTIONS

After providing a comprehensive overview of the history, pioneers, and specific techniques of hypnosis, here I would like to address the questions that I often hear when I introduce hypnosis and hypnotherapy. In fact, some of these questions were mine, too, when I studied hypnosis during my doctoral program. So here I review commonly asked questions to make sure that we remain on the same page when we think about hypnosis and its application for childbirth.

What Is Hypnosis?

The definition of hypnosis varies depending on the hypnotic tradition followed by the hypnotist. Some commonly accepted definitions include references to a natural, alerted state of consciousness (Yapko 1995), a relaxed state of mind (Lynn and Rhue 1991), and the state of concordance between body and mind (Flemons 2001). The Society of Psychological Hypnosis (a division of the American Psychological Association) defines hypnosis as "a state of consciousness involving focused attention and reduced peripheral awareness characterized by an enhanced capacity for response to suggestion" (psychologicalhypnosis.com/).

What Is Hypnotic Induction?

A procedure designed to induce hypnosis (APA, Division 30). Different approaches to hypnosis use different methods of induction. O'Hanlon (1992) describes four ways to achieve trance: spacing or de-focusing (a state between sleeping and waking up, also called the hypnogenic state); narrowing the spotlight (the attention is concentrated on one specific task, such as reading a book or driving a car); dissociation or splitting of awareness and activity (the attention is diffused using an activity such as playing a musical instrument, for example); and rhythmic or patterned behavior (for example, rocking).

What Is Trance?

According to Jay Haley (1993), "[the] trance state is usually defined as that moment of shift when the subject begins to follow suggestions involuntarily" (77). The trance state includes the possibility of such phenomena as amnesia (or forgetting), time distortion (expansion or contraction), age progression or age regression, anesthesia (lack of sensation), or analgesia (lack of pain) (O'Hanlon 1992).

What Is the Relationship between Hypnosis and Psychotherapy?

One of Erickson's students, Ernest Rossi, PhD, calls hypnosis the "mother of psychotherapy" (Zeig 2006). Hypnosis preceded many contemporary mental health interventions that have the common goal of introducing change by exploring and interacting with the client's feelings and sensations. Several psychotherapy techniques have roots in formal hypnosis. For example, a solution-focused technique that helps the therapist set goals for the session is inspired by the crystal ball technique used by Erickson. He invited his patients to look into the future where the problem no longer exists.

The use of specific hypnotic techniques in psychotherapy (such as Zeig's use of the client's minimal cues) is often called "hypnotherapy." Jay Haley (1993) described the goal of hypnotherapy as being to "change the behavior, sensory response, and consciousness of another person. A subsidiary goal is to extend that person's range of experience: to provide him with new ways of thinking, feeling, and behaving" (21).

What Is Self-Hypnosis?

Douglas Flemons (2001) compares self-hypnosis to the state of inner absorption. In fact, many authors writing about hypnosis suggest that any experience of hypnosis is an experience of self-hypnosis for the therapist and for the client.

What Is Mindfulness?

Jon Kabat-Zinn, MD, renowned teacher of mindfulness meditation, (2005) describes mindfulness as "the art of conscious living" (3). Instead of diffusing the attention as in hypnosis, in mindfulness a person aims to be highly aware of one's surroundings and one's emotional state in each moment. The aim of mindfulness is to cultivate our ability to be attentive to every moment, appreciating our life experience as it is and our interconnectedness with the world around us. Thus, mindfulness invites us to pay particularly close attention to the present moment without evaluating our experience, and rather than evaluating, becoming nonjudgmental of every moment we experience.

What Is Meditation?

Meditation offers a variety of possible ways to relate to our state of being, including an opportunity to experience mindfulness. It "helps us to wake up from this sleep of automaticity and unconsciousness, thereby making it possible for us to live our lives with access to the full spectrum of our conscious and unconscious possibilities" (Kabat-Zinn 2005, 3). Some say that hypnosis and meditation differ in their purpose. Some see hypnosis having a more concrete purpose, such as to stop smoking, lose weight, and so on, while the purpose of meditation is to reorient a person's experience of his surroundings. I cannot say that I completely agree with this description, since both hypnosis and meditation can result in the establishment of a different, more harmonious connection between the body and the mind, ultimately leading to the resolution of a presented problem. Where I see difference is in the individual versus collective experience: meditation invites the person to explore on their own, while hypnosis is a collaborative experience between at least two individuals.

What Is Suggestibility?

"Suggestibility is the person's ability to accept new ideas, new information" (Yapko 1995, 37). A good example outside of hypnosis comes from the world of advertising, where human suggestibility is carefully studied and manipulated. Unlike hypnosis, in advertising different possibilities are not offered or encouraged. However, in the case of psychotherapy, a person wants to change a behavior, thought, or emotion and then chooses a therapist to assist with this goal. By choice, the client has decided to follow specific suggestions to reach the desired changes. Thus, suggestibility is a necessary component for the successful outcome of therapy and hypnosis. It should not be confused with gullibility.

What Is Susceptibility?

This is a controversial topic. Some clinicians believe that susceptibility to suggestion is a constant trait, while others don't. The controversy matters because in order to create a successful hypnotic experience, the hypnotherapist must recognize that people are susceptible to different things. For a long time, clinicians believed that age influenced a person's susceptibility, for example, and that minors were the least susceptible to hypnosis. It was later discovered that children are as susceptible to hypnosis as adults, but manifest their hypnotic state differently. Adults usually become more relaxed, but children often experience fidgeting or agitation. It was also discovered that mental status was not relevant to a person's susceptibility: a person with dementia can be as susceptible as one without dementia. At one time research indicated that people with a higher

IQ were more susceptible, but recent studies link susceptibility with a greater ability to concentrate, often but not necessarily, a trait of an intelligent person. Multiple studies confirmed that the biggest factor in promoting susceptibility is the relationship between the client and the therapist (Yapko 1995).

Are Optimal Surroundings Necessary to Practice Hypnosis?

While some authors believe that hypnosis is best practiced in a calm, relaxed environment (Yapko 1995), practitioners of Ericksonian hypnosis do not advise introducing special conditions for hypnosis. This follows the logic of utilization, whereby a therapist uses specific components of a client's environment to promote trance, rather than trying to fit the environment into the client's preconceived notion about the hypnotic context. For example, sounds can be utilized as part of the hypnotic trance by integrating them into the trance induction. With this approach, hypnosis can be conducted in a variety of settings, including hospitals and operating rooms, where noises and bright light are part of the working environment.

In What Situations Is Hypnosis Not Advisable?

To use clinical hypnosis, clearance from the client's physician is recommended. Because mind and body are interconnected, and emotional states can contribute to illness, some conditions need to be treated by a physician who can target specific body and organ functions. For example, I was contacted by a person who was experiencing frequent headaches and wanted me to see her for hypnosis. When I talked to her doctor, I learned the person had been diagnosed with Lyme disease but refused to follow the prescribed treatment because she was convinced that hypnosis would be a miracle cure to save her from taking prescribed medications. Using hypnotic intervention in such a case would have been a disservice to the client. While I might have been successful in teaching her how to cope with the chronic headaches, the cause of headaches, Lyme disease, would not have been targeted and addressed. The illness would have progressed, while the person was managing one symptom. It is important to remember that hypnosis is a specific clinical intervention that should be practiced responsibly.

How Many Sessions Are Usually Needed for Hypnosis to Be Successful?

The answer is easy: it depends. It depends on the person, the presenting problem, the person's response to hypnosis, the person's ability to manage change, and so on. Because hypnosis is a highly individualized intervention, it is impossible to answer the question until a clinician has made a thorough assessment. That being said, it is true that Ericksonian hypnosis became the foundation for brief psychotherapy, in which usually twelve sessions are enough to produce change. So the estimate of sessions needs to consider whether the clinician draws on Ericksonian-based hypnosis and brief therapy models.

Who Is Qualified to Practice Hypnosis?

There is no central licensing board for practitioners of hypnosis. The requirements vary state by state, but usually include at least the requirement that clinicians practice hypnosis under the supervision of a licensed professional mental health or healthcare provider (for example, a medical doctor, licensed professional counselor, licensed mental health counselor, licensed marriage and family therapist, or licensed psychologist).

TWO

Pregnancy and Childbirth

Can any childbirth become a hypnobirth? Are natural childbirth and hypnobirth synonymous? What do we mean when we use the term "natural childbirth" and how do we counsel a patient about the pros and cons of hypnobirth? What are the historical artifacts and current cultural beliefs that guide expectant mothers' choices in their approach toward pregnancy and delivery? These and other questions will be addressed in this chapter.

HISTORY OF NATURAL CHILDBIRTH

What is natural birth? These two terms appear to be related: the word "birth" seems to invite the word "natural" just by its definition. After all, isn't it natural to give birth after being pregnant? In the contemporary medical environment, these combined concepts evoke a specific understanding of the birthing process, even though there are multiple ways to define these terms.

Providing the definition of natural birth, Gabriel (2011) points out a variety of meanings attached to this concept: vaginal birth, with or without the use of pharmaceutical drugs; birth without pain-relieving drugs; birth without any drugs whatsoever; birth with only select interventions allowed, according to the mother's birth plan; birth with the fewest interventions necessary to support the health of the mother and the baby— these are just a few options that expectant mothers and healthcare professionals mean when discussing natural birth.

However, a better understanding of the birthing context is required in order to understand how hypnosis can be helpful in preparation for and during natural birth. Thus, this chapter provides a brief overview of the history of natural childbirth in the United States and points out important milestones to understanding the past and present environment of birthing mothers, their healthcare providers, and the role of supportive aspects, including hypnosis.

Arnie and Neil (1982) distinguish three distinct stages in the history of childbirth in America from the nineteenth century to the present. These stages are closely related to the meaning attributed to pain and pain management accompanying labor. While before pain was seen as a natural and inseparable part of the birthing process, and birth itself was viewed as a revelatory, almost spiritual, experience, thinking changed in the nineteenth century, and pain was considered avoidable. Various means to control and relieve pain, such as chloroform and ether proposed by medical doctors prior to and during active labor, became available. The twentieth century brought the exploration of the subjective experience of pain during birth, by which the personal meaning of pain in a variety of contexts became significant. In her review of the history of childbirth, Gabriel (2011) proposes another stage, in the twenty-first century, of collaboration. This developed with the view of pain intervention that is meaningful to the mother, the child, and the mother's support system, including her healthcare team.

In this limited history of childbirth, the first shift from a "social childbirth philosophy" (pain is inevitable) to "medical illness model" that views pain as avoidable (Miller and Shriver 2012) happened with the introduction of the use of chloroform by Dr. Jay Simpson in 1847 and the use of ether by Dr. Walter Channing in 1848. Queen Victoria provided support to the concept of pain-free labor when she used chloroform in her births in 1853 and 1857. She claimed to be satisfied with the results (Ellis 2009). This conceptualization of the birthing process as a pain management enterprise prompted the introduction of specialized medical professionals on a birthing scene, replacing the non-invasive assistance of birthing partners such as doulas and midwives.

Beginning in the twentieth century, the scientific-medical framework became the predominant conceptualization of childbirth: labor was understood as a fundamentally medical process in which the optimal outcome depended on the use of medical skills and technology (Miller and Shriver 2012). The home birth became increasingly uncommon; most births were now happening in hospitals. Under general anesthesia, women became passive recipients of care administered by physicians, rather than active participants in their own labor. Thus, the mother became a primary patient: the importance of her experiences was not recognized and her emotions were considered an annoying complication in the work of the physician. The emotions and needs of the baby also were not considered and there was no room for the involvement of the mother's support system or the baby's family.

By 1930, obstetricians had become the primary healthcare providers involved in childbirth, completely eliminating the presence and perspective of midwives (Arnie and Neil 1982). These medical professionals, who had previously been trained to spot specific complications during pregnancy and childbirth, were now directing the whole process of the child birthing independent of the mother's previous experiences and current beliefs about pregnancy and the birthing process.

In 1933, British obstetrician Grantly Dick-Read published *Childbirth without Fear,* calling practitioners to recognize not only the physical but also the emotional part of the birthing process, as well as the influence of social and cultural perceptions of the mother in the resolution of pain (Arnie and Neil 1982). His work was seminal in the development of a bio-psychosocial perspective on the childbirth process, in which the connections between the body and the mind are recognized and explored. Dick-Read introduced the recognition that fear during labor can produce muscular tension in the uterine cervix, slowing the process of labor. He also introduced the concept of prenatal classes to prepare women for their birthing process by teaching them the anatomy and physiology of pregnancy and labor. Dick-Read also encouraged pregnant women to learn techniques of relaxation and invited birthing partners to attend birth. Being a physician, he did not deny the value of medical intervention. A firm believer that no one should be in pain, Dick-Read used small doses of morphine and chloral (or chloroform); however, his contribution to the exploration of body, mind, and social connections cannot be underestimated (Ellis 2009).

The work of Dick-Read opened the door to the exploration of the psychological side of the birthing process. In 1950 it was already recognized that pain is caused not only by stimuli but also by our psychological reactions to the stimuli. Applying this understanding to the experience of a mother in labor, it became important to explore each woman's understanding of the pain, her cultural and social background, values, and beliefs and her intrapersonal and interpersonal relationships (Arnie and Neil 1982). Obstetric care was transformed with this new attitude, and in the 1950s, local rather than general anesthesia was introduced. By this time, Clifford Lull and Robert Higson had published *Control of Pain in Childbirth* (1945), which introduced the awareness of the fetus as the second patient in the birthing room and raised the question of the influence of drugs transmitted through general and local anesthesia.

By the mid-twentieth century, women's psychological and subjective experiences were increasingly considered. In the 1960s, following the work of French physician Ferdinand Lamaze, who developed psychoprophylactic classes for expectant mothers and their partners, the Association of American Psychoprophylactic Obstetrics (ASPO) was first to organize classes developed and taught by medical educators. The classes introduced techniques for cognitive restructuring of ideas about birth and provided information on the anatomy of childbirth that deconditioned unhelpful information. In a sense, they taught women about the physiological transformation of their bodies in labor. Lamaze educators also recommended the participation of a coach, who would help the future mother deliver her baby with as little medical intervention as possible. Lamaze teachers encouraged parents to hold their baby immediately after the birth. This approach was strongly supported by both parents and nurses and contributed to the further development of the natural birth movement (Lowe and Frey 1983).

Underscoring the preeminence of women's desires and psychological experiences, the natural-birth movement flourished in the 1970s. It was characterized by less medicalized birth, the development of midwife-led birthing centers, involvement of birthing partners, appearance of labor lounges, creation of birthing pools, and the option to room-in (Jones 2012). It aimed to provide women with the sense of mastery (Arnie and Neil 1983).

While the natural birth movement brought many positive results and dramatically increased expectant mothers' choices pertaining to the birthing environment, it also had its downside. By emphasizing women's control during the birthing process, the movement at times minimized the unpredictability of birth itself. Thus, the movement contributed to the sharp disappointment of mothers who expected to give birth with minimal medical interventions but were unable to for a variety of reasons (Little et al. 2008). The movement also promoted, to some extent, the cult of the "natural" body and normative ideas about what "natural" means in the birth process (Jones 2012).

So how is natural birth regarded today? Addressing this question, Miller and Shriver (2012) examine current women's childbirth practices in the United States. While most of the women's choices are influenced by economic situations and the availability of birthing options, the authors also identified three distinct mindsets toward birthing: the scientific-medical framework, the religion-centered perspective, and the natural family perspective.

Women approaching delivery in a scientific-medical framework envision their birth in a hospital, supported by obstetricians as their preferred medical provider. They usually opt for a variety of medical interventions, among them epidural anesthesia, episiotomy, or elective C-section.

Women adopting the religion-centered view often seek minimal medical intervention, believing that women must suffer in labor to fulfill their role, which is constructed around punishment for Eve's sin. Women from these communities usually give birth at home, surrounded by midwives from the same religious community.

The natural family perspective on birth, the researchers found, "blends practices of voluntary simplicity and attachment parenting with elements of cultural feminism" (Miller and Shriver 2012, 712). Women with this point of view see "natural" birth as a social construction, where the meaning of the word depends on the context and the perspective of the person involved. As already pointed out by Gabriel (2011), for some women, natural birth means no professional assistance, no medication, no monitoring, and no attempt to control anything; at the other end of the spectrum, for other women natural birth refers to any type of vaginal birth. For all women seeing the world in the framework of the natural family perspective, "natural is constructed in opposition to technological, modern, processed, or corporate" (7). They adopt a labor-intensive and child-centered lifestyle, are skeptical about mainstream society's reliance on technology, and believe that medicine exists for profit. Similar to the earlier proponents of the natural birth movement, they conceptualize the safest birth as the one that relies on nature more that it relies on a technological intervention.

Thus, the role of culture on the conceptualization and practice of various types of natural and medicalized birth has become increasingly emphasized (Jones 2012). Not only do cultural ideas influence expectations of future mothers, they shape how the birth is perceived in a particular medical environment, the policies established in the country, and the available research and technology (Van Teijlingen, Wrede, Benoit, Sandall, and DeVries 2009). Today in the United States, almost every labor ends with an epidural, and a C-section is the most common surgery (Goer 1999). In fact, currently in the United States, cesarean sections make up 32 percent of all births, but only one-third of those are necessary to save a life. These numbers portray the present obstetric culture, which, compared to midwifery, indicates the dominance of medical intervention over supportive care.

Despite this highly medicalized culture, the movement of natural birth continues to evolve wherever the conversation continues about what constitutes the safest and the most satisfying birth for the mother and the baby. In fact, Gabriel's *Natural Hospital Birth* (2011) illustrates how the tenets of the natural birth movement can be implemented in a hospital environment. Gabriel not only states that a medical environment and a natural birth experience are not mutually exclusive, but also affirms that "a woman's commitment to natural birth does not end because she faces an emergency complication. It simply changes" (7). Because a commitment to one intervention does not necessarily exclude the panoply of others, a woman giving birth in a hospital still can have "the most instinctive, self-directed, intervention-free birth possible" (7), with the possibility of establishing "a physical, emotional, and spiritual relationship between a mother and a baby" (7). This approach represents a new way to consider natural birth options in a variety of contexts. In fact, it is not only the physical context that determines the possibility to have the most fulfilling birthing experience, it is also the emotional context the future mother is able to create in preparation and during the labor process that determines the successful outcome of her labor, no matter how the mother and healthcare providers define "successful."

A HISTORY OF HYPNOBIRTH

The use of hypnosis during pregnancy and childbirth goes back for more than a century (Brown and Hammond 2007; Abbasi, Ghazi, Barlow-Harrison, Sheikhvatan, and Mohammadyari 2009). However, the forms and purposes of the hypnotherapy varied greatly, depending on the philosophy of hypnosis of each practitioner. For example, in the 1940s, the American obstetrician Joseph DeLee was known to promote hypnosis during birth to achieve greater relaxation (Conkling 2002). In the 1960s, Dr. Santiago Roig-Garcia coined the term "hypnoreflexogenous method," which combined conditioned reflex with hypnosis and was used any time before, during, and after the active labor (Brown and Hammond). In this approach, expecting mothers were taught an active imagery technique while reinforcing the awareness that giving birth is a normal physiological act. Finally, in the 1990s, with the popularization of Marie Mongan's views, HypnoBirthing became a formalized approach with a specific philosophy of birthing and delivery. This chapter provides an overview of HypnoBirthing and a review of other recent uses of hypnosis in preparation for childbirth.

Inspired by work of Dr. Grantly Dick-Read (1933), the HypnoBirthing movement was built on Mongan's personal experience in childbirth and her desire to bring safe, comfortable, and satisfying birthing to every woman and newborn (Mongan 2005). An educator and hypnotherapist, Marie Mongan writes, "childbirth is a normal, natural and healthy function for women" (21), and sees it even as an extension of the sexuality of every man and woman, whereby the birthing of the child represents the ultimate act of love.

In her book *HypnoBirthing: The Mongan Method*, Mongan (2005) emphasizes that hypnobirth should be understood as an overarching philosophy of approaching pregnancy and birthing rather than a specific technique implemented during a particular time during active labor. Mongan writes, "birth is not about science; it's not about anatomy; it's not about doctors or midwives or nurses; it's not about who has control. It's about family—parents and their babies" (23). Thus, "a HypnoBirthing mother learns to embrace her body's innate knowledge of birthing, to relax into her birthing process, working *with* her body and her baby" (22). They are not learning about "*how* to birth," they are simply learning "*about* birth" (Mongan). Mothers are supported to have the most fulfilling and meaningful birth independent of the physical context chosen by the family (for example, birthing center or a hospital).

In fact, Mongan (2005) stresses the collaborative nature of the Hypno-Birthing movement, pointing out that the use of this philosophy neither precludes the use of medical interventions nor limits its use to women aiming to experience a vaginal birth. Since birth can take an unexpected turn, Mongan encourages all women to become familiar with the Hypno-

Birthing method, which, in her opinion, could help families remain calm as they face the many decisions and emotions associated with childbirth.

Mongan's method does not only address specific techniques that can be used during the first and second stages of labor, but also encourages women to explore mind-body connection (for example, by learning about their physiological responses to fear), and appreciate the power of the mind (for example, by introducing specific illustrations of how the words we use structure our way of thinking and apprehending information). Mongan's method also provides ways to build connections between the future parents and the baby. In fact, the role of the father is emphasized during pregnancy and the delivery. Finally, the method also encourages the future mother to build a support team that includes family and professional caregivers. The team is ultimately invited to be active participants, helping the mother birth her child.

To help the mother along the way, HypnoBirthing offers four major techniques: breathing, relaxation, visualization, and deepening. To achieve optimal results, future mothers are encouraged to practice these techniques well before the actual birth. During the HypnoBirthing classes, led by teachers certified in Mongan's method, the practice is first demonstrated and rehearsed. Then the patient and her birthing partner continue to practice at home.

The first technique is based on three types of breathing patterns. The first pattern, called Sleep Breathing, aims to introduce a state of relaxation to optimize such practices as guided imagery and visualization. The second pattern, Slow Breathing, is used specifically during the first stage of labor to stimulate the opening of the cervix and ease contractions (called "waves" in this approach). Finally, the third pattern, Birth Breathing, is used during the second stage of labor to help the actual birth of the baby. Expectant mothers are encouraged to master their breathing patterns first so they can get the most benefit from the next technique, relaxation.

Relaxation is taught through a variety of methods, with the understanding that some techniques work better for some people than others. Mongan (2005) discusses methods such as progressive relaxation, disappearing letters, light touch massage, and anchors. The techniques are first introduced by a trained practitioner. The woman can initiate some techniques herself, while others need the participation of the birthing partner. Again, the idea of regular practice long before the birthing day is emphasized. While Mongan's method can be implemented with a trained practitioner (for example, HypnoBirthing doula), during the labor itself, most of the techniques train the future mother to initiate self-hypnosis.

While the first two described techniques are viewed as fundamental building blocks of the HypnoBirthing, the third technique, Visualization, is designed to enhance the experience of breathing and relaxation and is mostly utilized in the first stage of labor. This includes the Opening Blossom (which likens the cervix to an opening rose), Blue Satin Ribbons (the cervix is visualized as soft blue satin ribbons), and the arm-wrist relaxation test. The Rainbow relaxation, also included in these visualizations, is not limited to use during labor. The expectant mother is taught to practice this every day, following a script and a provided CD.

Finally, the Deepening techniques are designed to enhance the efficacy of the Birth Breathing technique. This method helps birthing mothers achieve a very relaxed state that usually lasts until the baby is born. Some examples of the techniques are Glove Relaxation, the Depthometer, the Sensory Gate Valve, and Time Distortion. Again, the future mother is encouraged to practice Deep Relaxation long before labor and with the birthing companion.

Despite the existence of specific structured techniques, HypnoBirthing practitioners stress the importance of paying attention to everything surrounding the future mother before and during labor. Nutrition, exercise, birthing position, and a helpful, caring team are as important to a successful birth as any chosen technique.

Since the introduction of HypnoBirthing, several researchers have investigated the application of hypnosis as a supportive technique for expectant mothers (Brown 2007; Cyna and Andrew 2007; Mehl-Madrona 2004). While hypnotherapy can be used to manage a variety of symptoms common to future mothers before the labor (for example, early nausea and vomiting) and following the delivery (for example, postpartum depression and anxiety), most of the documented interventions refer to the management of anxiety and pain during the first and second stages of the birthing process: the opening of the cervix and the active birthing of the baby (Cyna et al. 2006; Mehl-Madrona 2004). For example, Brown and Hammond (2007) studied the beneficial and harmless use of hypnotic techniques to reduce pain in childbirth. Other research-proven benefits of hypnosis include increased self-confidence, increased calmness during labor, reduction of the cesarian section rate, control of elevated blood pressure and hyperemesis, prevention of premature delivery, and increased ease of transition into breastfeeding (Brown and Hammond 2007; Mehl-Madrona 2004).

The studies provide few details regarding any specific hypnosis approach to assist the mother in childbirth. Several studies mention self-hypnosis (Cyna and Andrew 2006; Werner, Uldbjerg, Zacariae, Rosen, and Nohr 2004), others mention problem-solving rather than insight-oriented hypnosis (Mehl-Madrona 2004), or point out specific hypnotic techniques, such as visualization or guided imagery (Abbasi et al. 2009). The way hypnosis is introduced to women also varies from study to study: Cyna and Andrew (2006) taught hypnotic techniques for up to four sessions, each lasting between forty and sixty minutes after thirty-five weeks' gestation, while Werner et al. (2009) provided three group trainings of one hour each over three consecutive weeks. In comparison to the HypnoBirthing method, these researchers seem to focus on specific techniques of hypnosis rather than the encompassing philosophy of mindful living, in which hypnosis is one contributing part of the future mother's experience. Nonetheless, all but one of the reviewed studies mentions the potential benefit of the chosen hypnotic intervention (Werner's research did not support nor deny the benefits of hypnosis in childbirth).

Cyna and Andrew (2006) note that their findings demonstrate that "nulliparous women taught self-hypnosis had a lower rate of utilization of epidural analgesia and decreased requirements for labor augmentation with oxytocics compared with the population not taught self-hypnosis" (467). In addition, "two women required C-section, but reported that they found self-hypnosis useful for relaxation and that it enhanced a sense of control during both anesthesia and surgery" (467). Mehl-Madrona (2004) highlighted that hypnosis appeared to improve the likelihood of uncomplicated birth. Brown and Hammond (2007) underscored the fact that more than 60 percent of women using hypnosis in the study were able to deliver without medications or anesthesia. Finally, the study by Abbasi et al. (2009) revealed that the use of hypnotherapy increased satisfaction, sense of control, and confidence; reduced fear, anxiety, and labor pain; produced shorter labor; reduced tiredness; and increased consciousness. Ultimately, the woman's whole attitude toward childbirth shifted, resulting in a more spiritual perception of the birthing event.

Reflecting on these findings, it seems clear that much still needs to be done to explore the mechanism and benefits of hypnosis in childbirth. However, the conclusion of Bobart and Brown (2002, as cited by Brown and Hammond 2007) is significant. Considering the influence of hypnotherapy on expectant mothers, they write, "The most important five minutes of our lives are the first five minutes after birth. How quickly we adapt to extra-uterine life often determines how quick we are the rest of our lives. We are missing a tremendous opportunity by not making hypnosis available to all our obstetrics patients. They and their newborn infants have so much to gain, so little to lose" (1).

THREE

Special Connections

Hypnosis can be conceptualized as a unique means to connect our mind, body, and spirit to alter our experiences and sensations. Rather than seeing such connections as unusual and mysterious, we can examine them in a larger framework of systems-based research and practice, which emphasizes the relational understanding of the world rather than a linear cause and effect interpretation of events. Circular causality takes then the precedents in our interpretations and allows us to account for multiple possibilities and viewpoints opening multiple ways to understand and account for a particular phenomenon. Systems thinking is contagious, in that once we start seeing how we are all interconnected, it is quite hard to avoid seeing these connections. In this chapter we examine the history of systems-based concepts and explore how hypnosis can establish one of the most meaningful and long-lasting connections, that between a mother and her child.

MINDS, BODIES, AND SPIRITS

In the past twenty-five years, much has been written about systems-based philosophy and the interconnections between the body, mind, and spirit of patients and their families when applied to a medical context (Bateson 2000; Engel 1977; Kenney 2002; Hodgson, Lamson, Mendenhall, and Crane 2014). However, the dualistic approach, in which physical sensations are considered apart from emotions, is still the dominant metaphor in the contemporary Western medical environment. When I ask myself how such an attitude continues to persevere, I have to acknowledge it is more appealing to healthcare practitioners. Viewing the world as a causal chain of events, in which one can determine the cause of a broken chain just by finding the damaged piece, may seem logical,

31

but it can be simplistic in the realm of healthcare and mental health problems. Although the first solution might seem the correct one, by being open to other possibilities, one can find a multitude of interrelated causes that might contribute to the problem.

Consider the following example. An expectant mother goes to a physician, who tells her that if she doesn't relax more, she will be at risk for a premature delivery. When the woman returns for the next visit, the physician discovers that nothing has changed in the mother's approach to self-care. The physician deduces that the patient is resistant to his recommendations and is unable to change. The physician might also assume the patient does not respect his authority or does not know how to relax and needs more guidance in self-care. All of these options might be true; however, the physician can't successfully change the patient's behavior if he does not learn what the patient is doing and/or find out about her particular beliefs and understandings about what she was doing. By asking more questions rather than offering more advice, the physician can achieve multiple goals: he can connect with the patient by establishing not only his authority but also his caring attitude; find out what an *acceptable* solution for the patient is, and provide specific guidelines that fit the patient's beliefs and perceptions. By acknowledging that the patient's actions are often influenced by her emotions and values, the physician recognizes the interconnected web of the patient's experiences, which opens the door for a more successful intervention.

Most people do not recognize the powerful connections between their bodies, minds, and spirits. Statements such as "I have a sore back," or "today my anxiety is over the top," illustrate how we often separate our physical sensations from our emotional experience. Often this helps us make sense of our experience and think of an intervention to ease our pain or discomfort. If there is a physical cause, one set of actions is considered; if the cause is related to emotions, another set of actions is preferred. However, such separation can be misleading as well. In fact, in many cultures including subcultures in America informed by systems thinking, the interventions considered the most effective are those that simultaneously address the interplay of our body, mind, and spirit.

Hypnosis is just one of the interventions that builds on the bio-psychosocial-spiritual connections identified by a systems-based approach—a scientifically based method of intervention that has been around for almost a century.

The earliest pioneers of systems thinking were American philosopher Paul Weiss and Austrian-born biologist Ludwig von Bertalanffy. Both authors underlined the importance of considering the relationship among different levels of any system rather than only its isolated parts. Instead of considering the system as a static entity, they taught that one should explore how the entity was created and maintained. For instance, in systems thinking, a family is not made up only of a mother, father, and daughter, but of the *relationships between and among everyone who makes up the family*. If we take a pregnant woman's fears as an example, not only should caregivers look at how to reduce the fears, but also they should look at how she and those around her (family) perceive the fears and their understanding of the fears. So in systems thinking, her fear is not an entity in itself to be isolated and treated, but is part of a system of many parts, the interrelationships of which need to be considered.

A doula once told me about a mother who was worried because her pregnant daughter had elected not to have an epidural. The mother's perception was that her daughter was weak and "emotional," and the mother was worried that the daughter would not receive enough medical support to have a safe labor. In fact, the mother believed that the daughter was taking too much on herself, which would result in failure on her part. The doula explained to me that the family had a Latino cultural background, and her concern was common among older women in that culture.

In contrast, I recently met another family in which the mother was worried about her daughter's decision to have an epidural. The mother could not understand why her daughter needed a medical intervention for an act that has been performed for thousands of years without help from a doctor. This family was from Russia, where local anesthesia was not used regularly, especially when an older woman was delivering the child.

An understanding of the cultural context not only helps us acknowledge special rituals and traditions surrounding birth, it helps us understand the different intra- and interpersonal connections and how they can affect the expectant mothers' experiences before and during childbirth. In these cases, knowing the different perceptions of the families helped me explore the daughters' beliefs about a safe birth and calm the mothers' anxieties generated by the daughters' decisions. The end result was that the mothers and daughters were able to reestablish stronger connections, which will help the mothers support their daughters in labor.

Following Weiss and von Bertalanffy, many researchers and clinicians contributed to the development of systems-based thinking. Chemist Ilia Prigogine (1918–2003), anthropologist Gregory Bateson (1904–1980), linguist Bela Banathy (1919–2003), and Chilean biologist Humberto Maturana (1928) were among those who advanced theories related to systems thinking. Their applications spread across disciplines of engineering, biology, philosophy, social sciences, and literature. Applied to the medical setting, they promoted a more holistic patient-centered and individualized approach to healthcare, in which the needs of the patient and the doctor's interconnection with systems such as caregivers and family members were considered of utmost importance for the most successful care.

Hypnotherapy builds on and strengthens this recognition of the connections between our mind, body, and emotions, and their importance in
childbirth. It invites the future mother to perceive her experience from a
systems point of view, recognizing the interconnections between her sensations, feelings, and beliefs and those of others surrounding her. In fact,
in families it is often impossible to differentiate whose sensation created a
particular emotional climate (Kerr and Bowen 1988). Just by acknowledging the interconnectivity, we are taking the first step of the exploration.

By conceptualizing hypnosis as a travel guide that leads the patient
through a land of sensations and emotions without frontiers, caregivers
help their patients develop a particularly respectful attitude toward their
bodies, minds, and spirits. Through hypnosis, patients are encouraged to
explore what might constitute discomfort, what contributes to positive
sensations, and what constitutes a valuable experience during pregnancy,
delivery, and the first moments with the baby. Nonetheless, in order to
engage in such exploration, both a patient and a healthcare provider need
to adopt a curious attitude of openness to exploring various possibilities.
In fact, openness to experience is one of the prerequisites to exploring
different connections within and outside.

These uses of hypnosis do not need to wait for the actual birth. They
can establish the connections and start utilizing the patient's insights to
the benefit of the future baby and the caregivers. It seems that once the
expectant mother and her doctor can see themselves as part of a larger
web, they cannot return to an attitude of isolation. It's like the Gestalt
image of what at first appears to be a young woman, but on closer examination, an old woman becomes apparent. At that point, most people can
no longer see the young woman.

When I was pregnant, I became highly aware of how my body affects
my mind. So I became curious about everything I was doing, eating,
drinking, and experiencing and how these body- and mind-guided experiences affected my pregnancy and my developing baby. I started to explore what I enjoyed doing, what brought comfort, what was stressful,
what was anxiety provoking, what was calming. I invited different sensations and explored all of them and remembered some of them. I was
struck by the connections and made an effort to keep in mind what
worked for me. Thus, I followed Mongan's advice to start practicing early
in the birthing process; at the same time, I did it with a playful mindset.
That helped reestablish connections that were starting to fade and create
new connections to explain other experiences while I was expecting.
Thus, I used hypnosis as another medium to establish connections with
myself, with my future baby, with my physician, and with the world
around us.

MOTHER AND CHILD

When I share with people that I used hypnosis to give birth to my child, I am often asked what prompted me. While a multitude of reasons contributed to my decision, two primary motives led to my decision: my attempt to protect my child from any unnecessary medical intervention and my eagerness to welcome my child into the world in the warmest possible way. While it was impossible to predict how my birth would occur, I wanted to set the stage for the most calm, hospitable birth. Believing Mongan's view of birth as constituting the ultimate fulfillment of love between the two parents, I wanted my daughter to feel most welcomed by her father and me into this new strange world. I also believed that the experience of birthing itself could establish a strong connection between a mother and her child. Giving the baby and the parent(s) the possibility to connect facilitates attachment and promotes the creation of a strong bond between the mother and the child.

Mila and Jon Kabat-Zinn (1998) tell a story related to this in their wonderful book *The Inner Work of Mindful Parenting*. An elderly lady, reflecting on her experience giving birth in the 1960s, describes being alone in the hospital, unconscious while she gave birth, deprived of the chance to see her child right after giving birth. She had a hard time even realizing that she had given birth to her son. Disconnected from her own experience of having been an expecting and then a birthing mother, she had difficulty connecting with her son and her new role of mother.

The connection with the newborn ultimately happens through the connection that the expecting mother establishes with herself and her own experiences and the meanings of these experiences for her. You can discuss with your patients/clients the following questions to encourage self-discovery during pregnancy. They will be helpful in choosing meaningful and beneficial hypnosis techniques.

- What are your hopes, dreams, and goals as an expectant mother and as a woman in general? What were you planning to achieve but never did? What makes you sad, happy, and proud?
- What does it mean to you to be pregnant? What is your image of a successful pregnancy?
- What does it mean to you to be in labor? How do you envision a successful labor? What does you expect from yourself?
- How do you envision the first encounter with your child? What will it mean to hear the first sound of your child, to touch your child, to see your child? How will the birth of your child affect your first interactions with your child? What will you be able to do, not be able to do?

- How does the environment in which you are giving birth influence your perceptions and shape your experience? What environment do you envision when you think about giving birth?
- What does the birthing experience tell you about yourself, the system in which you live, the relationships you have with your loved ones?

It is by engaging in self-examination that the future mother will be able to make a strong connection with her child. To help her, you can also ask what her image of a successful birth is and even further what her vision of a successful relationship with her child is. What message would she like to transmit to her child? What would she like to teach her child? Using hypnosis as part of the preparation for the birthing process offers an opportunity for the woman to stop and reflect, connecting with her own perceptions, beliefs, and sensations and to build on them to achieve a more fulfilling life experience.

Describing childbirth, Mila and Jon Kabat-Zinn (1998) write, "Birthing is a process in which, like parenting, each situation, and veritably, each moment, brings a different challenge. At times we meet it fully. At other times we may retreat, close down, go on automatic pilot. There may be times when we completely lose it, or find ourselves complaining and cursing and rejecting what feels like a miserable experience" (162). Birthing is a human experience that can be viewed as potential for personal growth and maturity. Birthing does not have to be perfect but can be regarded as another opportunity for the mother to connect with her experiences as a human in the most primitive term of that word, with no pretending, enhancing, or acting; to connect in order to learn about herself and consequently about her baby. The first connection that she makes with her baby will be the most genuine and will impact her ability to relate to her child in the future. Birth is just the beginning (Kabat-Zinn and Kabat-Zinn)! It is the beginning of furthering a connection with ourselves and with other human beings. Hypnosis can be used as a means to that end.

Reflecting on how we introduce our beliefs and values to our children, Kabat-Zinn and Kabat-Zinn (1998) write, "Just as we cannot impose values of peace and harmony in the family, we cannot inculcate values, such as generosity, compassion, non-harming, equality, and appreciation for diversity through moralizing or coercion. We can advocate for them however, but ultimately, it is through *embodying* these values ourselves that our children come to have a direct experience of them and absorb them into their view of themselves and the world" (235). The word "embodiment" particularly stands out. With every gesture we are transmitting a powerful message to our child. It is a complicated dance as we are teaching the choreography every minute of the dance: when we are in a good or bad mood, when we are happy or sad, when we are exhausted or energized, we do not stop teaching. What message are we transmitting to our child when telling his birth experience? What message does the child receive fresh out of the womb? What does he or she feel? What do we feel? What do we feel together with our child? As "relationships are built on shared moments" (Kabat-Zinn and Kabat-Zinn 1998, 240), what experiences do we create during pregnancy and birth?

Hypnosis helps us connect our bodily sensations with emotional experiences by establishing meaningful relationships. Despite the common belief that trance allows a person to disconnect from pain and other sensations by being in a sleep-like state, hypnosis does quite the opposite. It allows the person to be very aware of the surroundings, but in a different, more meaningful way. When expectant mothers connect with themselves, they are then able to establish a meaningful relationship with their child. This is not to minimize uncomfortable or painful sensations sometimes associated with the birthing process. However, you can invite expectant mothers to relate the sensations to the context of giving birth, which is quite different from the context of having a headache after an exhausting day. The outcome of the birthing process is the beginning of a new experience; the process of the birth is related to the natural transformation of the woman's body in order to accommodate the birthing itself; the welcoming of the baby and of parenthood is the end goal of the birthing process, which sets the stage for the development of future relationships.

In that act of giving life, healthcare providers can play a crucial role providing guidance and helping the future mother to explore her own abilities as well as different resources that can enhance her experience of a successful childbirth. Hypnosis, with its inclusive philosophy and specific techniques, is just one way to encourage future mothers to explore their own expectations of themselves and of the surrounding world. My own experience illustrates how such exploration can be initiated by using hypnotic techniques long before the actual birth.

As long as I can remember my ideal picture of birth, I always wanted to give birth in the water. When I was pregnant, I realized that because I was planning to give birth in a hospital, I would not have that opportunity, because hospitals in my region did not have accommodations for water birth. So I worked throughout my pregnancy on visualizing the water and imagining my sensations when I am in the water. By my due date, I was able to feel the muscle relaxation that I usually feel in the water just by thinking about the water. In fact, I could even smell the water, feel it on my fingers and even feel the breeze from the ocean when I thought about it. This technique, called "anchoring" in Mongan's method, was helpful to evoke a relaxing context during my birthing process. It is interesting that even by thinking about the ocean now, I can still feel the same sensations.

Hypnosis encourages women to see birth not as a separate act, but as a culmination of our experiences as an expecting mother. By starting to practice hypnosis early during her pregnancy, the mother can explore what is comfortable, what is disturbing, and what is painful. It also allows her to establish connections with different layers of her experiences. These connections will be used later during the childbirth. Since I had discovered early that water was a relaxing environment, I was able to practice my visualization to establish the anchoring of water and evoke it during the childbirth. This allowed me to be comfortable enough to become curious not only about my own experiences, but also about the experiences of my baby who was being born. I was so powerfully connected to my experience that I was able to take ownership of my experiences. I did not feel that the birthing was happening to someone else and I was just a visitor. On the contrary, I felt that I, as well as my baby, was an active participant.

Every future mother will have her own way to find relaxation and comfort. Each woman will also have her own way to relate to and connect with her baby. There is no right or wrong way to do it. The most important thing is that she becomes aware of the importance of her connections. Some mothers will have to have medical interventions to ensure their own health or the health of their baby. This need not prevent them from establishing connections. By helping women conceptualize birth as the last page of the *Pregnancy Book* and the first page of the *Baby Book*, you can invite a woman to use everything that she learned about herself during pregnancy and everything that she would like to see in her future child while she is giving birth. By using hypnosis techniques built on her past experiences and present sensations, she will transform her present experience.

FOUR

Hypnotic Mindset

The months before birth are filled with preparation and expectations. The future mother and her family are envisioning the birth and are getting ready to welcome the baby into the world. By taking time to explore this vision along with the family and the expectant mother, a healthcare practitioner can achieve multiple goals: a better understanding of the patient's perception of a successful birth, a unique opportunity to participate in the creation of this vision by sharing his expertise, and many opportunities to provide reassurance to the future mother and her loved ones. By taking time to ask a few simple questions, a provider sets strong foundations for a successful collaboration by becoming an important member of the birthing team.

CREATING A VISION

The language surrounding the childbirth process can create a business-like atmosphere in which the future parents end up expecting that the pregnancy is nothing more than a series of hurdles they have to overcome. For example, just notice how often the words "management" and "method of delivery" are used in the vocabulary of caregivers when speaking with future mothers. By using this language, healthcare providers may create an expectation among parents and healthcare providers that childbirth is little more than an allusion to effective pain management.

Yet, reflecting on the parents' expectations before and after the birth, Kabat-Zinn and Kabat-Zinn (1998) address the possibility that pregnancy can be viewed as a transitional period during which the expecting mother and those around her can contemplate the transformations and different changes that accompany pregnancy. Often our busy American schedule does not allow time for such reflection: many expecting mothers continue to work almost till the end of their pregnancy. However, despite the scarcity of time for meditation and contemplation, each woman needs to find ways to ponder the significant changes that will soon transform her and her family's existence.

Acknowledging the changes about to occur relates also to the cultural and family rituals that accompany the transition time. Different traditions mark their unique understandings of the childbirth process and expectations of the birth itself. The now-traditional baby shower is a widespread ritual in the United States. However, in Russia, for example, it is considered bad luck to buy or set up anything for a baby that has not yet been born. My Latino and Jewish friends say that a similar view was once held in their cultures, as well. However, in the recent economic crisis, the baby shower has become more widely accepted even in the cultures that initially rejected it. It just makes sense to accept help with all the expenses. Economic influences play an important role in structuring our traditions, values, and behaviors regarding the childbirth process. It is important to remember and acknowledge this influence, among many others, within the culture and traditions in our lives.

Because we cannot separate ourselves from cultural and other influences (Aceros 2012; Gergen 2009), mental health and healthcare providers, as well as expecting women, would do well to become aware of this impact and its influence on their views, understandings, and expectations. With curiosity, both the clients and the care providers can ask questions such as, "Who are we?" "What is our core foundation?" and "What fundamental life principles shape our approach to our daily routine tasks as well as special events such as childbirth?" The answers set the stage for the caring involvement of healthcare providers with their patients and clients (including hypnotic work pertaining to the childbirth). They establish at least a preliminary framework for the vision of the childbirth process of everyone involved.

Instead of attempting to provide "objective care" with a "neutral" mindset, as the healthcare provider, you may benefit by reflecting on how your upbringing, your values, and your beliefs about a safe childbirth influence your care for your patients. Stop for a minute and ask yourself, "What made me ask this specific question at this specific time?" "Why am I curious to hear this specific story?" "How does what the person just told make me feel?"

By acknowledging your own inspirations and biases, you are able to work with them instead of against them. You are acknowledging that just by touching or looking at another person you change them. To paraphrase famous psychotherapist and communication expert John Weakland, "We cannot *not* be making any difference." However, we can become highly aware of what kind of difference we are making and consider whether it is in line with what the patient is expecting us to do.

Since we all have different influences and experiences in our lives, our vision of a successful childbirth will be different as well. Many authors have celebrated and normalized these differences (Kabat-Zinn and Kabat-Zinn 1998; Mongan 2005). Reflecting on the parents' support in the process of the childbirth and delivery, England and Horowitz (1998) note, "Parents deserve support for any birth option which might be right for them" (xiii). The question is: What is the most effective use of hypnotherapy to support parents and expectant mothers in creating their vision?

Milton Erickson used a technique called the "crystal ball," in which he invited his patients to look at or imagine a crystal ball and consider how the present problem might be resolved in the future (de Shazer 1985). With this technique, Erickson demonstrated his assumption that the client already knows the answer and will be able to use it when resolving the problem in the future. Erickson inspired the hypnotic work of Steve de Shazer (De Jong and Kim Berg 2012; de Shazer and Dolan 2007), who, like Erickson, used informal trance-inducing techniques. De Shazer talked to his clients in such a way as to lead them into a trance-like state.

This informal trance through conversation can be used with a future mother during the birthing process. For example, to create a vision of a successful birth, the healthcare provider can use a modified version of de Shazer's "Miracle Question" (de Shazer and Dolan 2007). It would go like this:

"Try considering a rather strange question. . . . The strange question is this. . . . After you finish reading this sentence, you will go back to your work (home, school) and you will do whatever you need to do the rest of today, such as taking care of the children, cooking dinner, watching TV, giving the children a bath, and so on. . . . It will be time to go to bed [think of specific circumstances that apply to your patient's daily routine]. Everybody in your household is quiet, and you are sleeping in peace. In the middle of the night, a miracle happens, and you are able to envision the birth of your child, as you would like it to happen. . . . But because this happens while you and everyone in your household is sleeping, you have no way of sharing your vision with your loved ones. . . . So, when you wake up tomorrow morning, what do you want to share with everyone in your house (with your loved ones or your birth partner)? What details from your dream will you share with your loved ones? What was happening in it? . . . Who was present? . . . What were they doing? . . . What were you doing? Imagine that you were able to film a little movie of it. . . . Try to describe with as many details as possible specific scenes from the movie."

This technique helps the future mother envision goals, and like Erickson's technique, rests on the assumption that the client or patient already has a specific answer and will be able to articulate it with a professional's help. If you are a healthcare provider asking the questions, speak slowly, matching the breathing pattern of your client or patient. Also, be mindful not to "rescue" your clients too soon by providing an answer. Give time for the person to ponder the question. It is also important to follow up with more questions to get as many details as possible.

There are many variations on the Miracle Question. For example, England and Horowitz (1998) ask an expectant mother, "When you think about being in labor, what image comes to mind? How does it feel for you to be giving birth?" (50). In this case, a visualization technique is utilized to help expectant mothers to envision their future birth. England and Horowitz also use a technique called the "Door to Birth," in which they ask the future mother, "If there were a secret door to birth, to giving birth, what would it look like? What's behind it, around it, or in front of it? Is anyone in the picture?" (53). In this case, while the question asked is similar, the aspect of trance (present in Erickson's and de Shazer's questions) is missing. Nonetheless, these questions can help expectant mothers not only to determine the components of a successful birth that are important to her, but also to articulate how she envisions accomplishing them. However, asking a question in a trance-inviting way may help the mother concentrate better on her thoughts and sensations and ultimately produce a more concrete, detailed answer.

The "Miracle Question" and the "Door to Birth Question" should be the starting point for an exploration of the mother's vision. After asking the questions, do not rush to wrap up the conversation, but spend some time exploring the details of the answers by asking clarifying questions. The answers will deepen the vision, including bringing out specific actions needed for the desired future. This technique is empowering for both the client and the provider because it provides a starting point for a collaborative endeavor in which the mother can guide the practitioner in the exploration of her vision of the childbirth.

These hypnotic techniques illustrate again how important it is to help the mother start thinking about the birth even at the beginning of her pregnancy. In the same way that the examples above helped create the vision of the successful birth, any pregnant woman can be helped to create a vision of her successful pregnancy. It is important to emphasize that the use of these techniques does not assume that the pregnancy or the birth will occur exactly as the woman envisions it. However, by helping the patient reflect on her pregnancy and her vision of the birthing process, providers can develop a list of her priorities and what will make her birth special to her, even if her vision requires certain modifications and interventions to keep her and her baby safe.

MAKING A PLAN

One of the characterizing features of the natural childbirth movement is its goal of empowering women to be in charge of their own bodies, decisions, and experiences. Several key figures of the movement, such as Lamaze (Jones et al. 2012; Karmel 2005), Gaskin (2003), and Mongan (2005), believed that women needed to be educated not so much about available technological options as about their own anatomy and the natural structures designed to enable them to give birth. The movement celebrates the wisdom of women's bodies and assumes that with enough information about their bodies' natural abilities, women will be more at ease and even consider birthing without specific medical interventions.

In addition to considering their bodies' abilities, women and caregivers are encouraged to approach birth from a highly individualized and personalized perspective: each birth as a unique experience for the mother. The messages to the mothers are, "No one birth is like another," and "Each mother should consider what constitutes a special, safe, desirable birth for her."

To achieve this unique birth experience, mothers are encouraged to plan their birth in advance and to make sure that every one of their healthcare team is aware of their wishes. One common way to make this happen is for the mothers to create a Birth Plan, which includes specific details pertaining to their birthing process (for example, medical interventions not acceptable to them, those who may accompany them during the childbirth, and how they want the infant to be treated in the few seconds after the baby is born).

Birth plans have varied tremendously from one birthing philosophy to another. The titles of the documents differed, illustrating the multitude of existing birthing approaches. For example, Mongan (2005) refers to the "Birth Preference Sheets," encouraging women not only to enumerate their desired attitudes during childbirth, but also to compose a letter to the main healthcare provider describing their chosen birthing philosophy. Sears and Sears (1994), on the other hand, teach future mothers to include in their written plan such topics as pain management, birth location, and post-birth instructions.

Practitioners who encourage their patients to write a birth plan see it as an important communication between the patient and the healthcare provider (Sears and Sears 1994; Simkin 2013). Before finalizing the plan, an expectant mother is encouraged to engage in a conversation about it with the physician-obstetrician or the midwife. They also see the plan as a form of test by the expectant mother of the healthcare provider, asking him about the most common procedures he usually performs and his philosophy of care.

Since their appearance, birthing plans have become popular among pregnant women in general and no longer constitute the hallmark of the natural childbirth movement. In fact, the American Pregnancy Association promotes pregnancy wellness by encouraging women to engage in powerful, positive thinking about the birth and to create a Birth Plan in which they indicate their preferences of the setting and treatments used during the delivery (www.americanpregnancy.org/).

Despite the flexible aspects of the Birth Plan technique, some professionals approach it with caution, and others oppose the creation of Plans, fearing the rigidity of the document might lock the future mother in her expectations and prevent a healthcare provider from intervening when needed (England and Horowitz 1998). England and Horowitz call the Birthing Plan a "trap," leading the mother to focus too much on external forces she cannot control, rather than on her own inner experiences. They insist, "In writing a birth plan, a woman focuses on fending off outside forces which she fears will shape her birth. This effort distracts her from trusting herself, her body, and her spirituality. Rather than planning her own hard work and surrender, her energy is diverted toward controlling the anticipated actions of others" (97). These authors also mention the fact that while a Birthing Plan might seem unique to the expectant mother, it might seem trivial and generic to an experienced healthcare provider, who could overlook the unique wishes carefully articulated by the future mother. England and Horowitz caution that instead of generating a meaningful conversation, the Birthing Plan can evoke irritation in healthcare providers, preventing a fruitful collaboration.

My perspective on the pros and cons of writing a birthing plan lies within the framework of a hypnobirth and focuses on two considerations related to the plan: language and systems.

I have already discussed one of the essential elements of Ericksonian hypnosis: the ability to speak the patients' language so that they feel they know what the caregiver means and that what he means is beneficial for them. They feel that he understands them. Erickson's patients trusted his sincere concern and hopefulness in the positive resolution of their specific issues. These beliefs and trust were established by Erickson and later Ericksonian hypnotists through the use of specific words crucial for such communication.

Language is also important for the future mother's communication with the provider. While she might think that a Birthing Plan would be a good way to explore the provider's philosophy of care and to communicate her wishes about the birth, she may not know the most effective way to convey her thoughts. In fact, without knowing the nuts and bolts of the medical system, expectant mothers are hard-pressed to compose a meaningful message to a care provider.

Because it is important to choose the words (as did Erickson) that will establish communication and trust with a healthcare provider, the conversation between mother and provider will be more effective if it is initiated by a medical provider rather than a layperson. Healthcare providers are in a unique position to initiate a meaningful conversation that can help both the patient and the provider to get to know each other's visions, beliefs, hopes, and fears. Providers know the medical system, have experienced many births, yet treat each birth as a unique experience, and they are aware of the range of possibilities and limitations of available technologies. Such a conversation might start by exploring the future mother's vision, as discussed in the previous chapter, while at the same time educating her about what may be possible or impossible to achieve in a specific medical context (e.g., birthing center vs. hospital). In this way, a Birthing Plan can be created with a medical provider as a result of conversation rather than a result of a one-sided deliberation on a subject in which the person may not be well versed.

If a healthcare professional agrees to engage in such a conversation, several rules need to be respected:

- No question is stupid: encourage the patient to ask you any question, even the one that might appear stupid or trivial.
- Do not look at your watch when talking to your patient: this is an unusual kind of conversation in a medical world in which each second is precious and to be guarded. Plan the conversation ahead and spend as much time as necessary to answer all the questions. Consider this time as an investment in the trust between you and your patient.
- Do not use medical jargon or fancy technical words. They might make the client shy to ask a question. Try to use the patient's language as much as possible (even the same words) and summarize what your patient says to make sure that you understand her.
- When addressing the Birthing Plan, point out the discrepancy between the fluidity and unpredictability of a birth and a rigid checklist. Engage the patient in a conversation about prioritizing and compromising. Help her to consider the sentences in the plan not as concrete but as drops of rain, the amount of which may vary from creating a puddle or a little river. Some puddles will dry out, while others will expand. Consider talking to a patient about the plan as baby steps toward the unknown and somewhat frightening world of giving birth to another human being.
- Finally, instead of just listening to what an expectant mother does not want to do, help her to articulate what she does want, instead. A positive framework can provide your patient with a sense of direction much more effectively than a negative statement that offers no alternative.

While engaging in a conversation, both the client and provider need to keep in mind that a Birthing Plan is similar to a treatment plan: overall goals and interventions are articulated with an opportunity to be adjusted moving forward. Nothing is rigid, but fluid, changing, and transforming, as the birth itself.

BUILDING A TEAM

When I worked in a hospice setting, I practiced as a social worker on a team made up of a physician, a nurse, a chaplain, a volunteer, and myself. Together we strived to make the last moments of terminally ill people and their families the most memorable, the least terrifying, and the most peaceful (whatever those specific words meant for each family) as possible. I often experienced the powerful presence of our team that arose because what one person could never have done alone was accomplished in a collaborative effort. In fact, the patient and the family were considered an important part of the team, because it was they who determined the goals and influenced the treatment plan. They guided us with their definitions of a "good death," and if we listened carefully, we were able to make a significant difference in these people's lives.

I have often thought how incredibly sad it was that we had to wait till the end of our lives to be connected to a team of professionals who care deeply and know how to work together. Most of my experience with healthcare had been one of misunderstandings and lack of collaboration, which blocked any continuity of care. When I became pregnant, I hoped to create a team that would assist me during my childbirth. I quickly discovered that it was easier said than done.

My Physician

My usual OBGYN was still practicing gynecology but not obstetrics. When she informed me that I was pregnant, she also told me that she could refer me to a practicing obstetrician who would monitor my pregnancy and delivery. Despite the fact that today expectant mothers have a variety of birthing options, my OBGYN assumed that I would opt for a hospital delivery. While the choice was in line with my expectations, when I look back at it today, I can see how the OBGYN did not give me an opportunity to make an educated choice about where I would like to birth my baby. In an ideal situation, my OBGYN would have presented me with a variety of possibilities, explaining that the delivery did not have to happen in a hospital, but could happen in a birthing center or even at home. Knowing my personality, I probably would still have opted for birth in a hospital. However, it is important for healthcare providers to explore the wishes of the patients and to design future interventions incorporating these wishes into the care plan. Such a strategy actually promotes compliance with the proposed treatment plan and assures better continuity of care (Engel 1977).

At that time, I was not aware of many birthing options, which ranged from having an obstetrician help me through birthing in a hospital to having a midwife assist me in a home-based delivery. I thought my only choice was help from available doctors. So I decided to look for a physician whose philosophy of care was in line with my philosophy of birth. Since I knew that I would practice hypnosis during the birthing process, I looked for a professional who would assist me by offering similar techniques and embracing my way of approaching birth.

After I shared my thoughts with my OBGYN, she recommended a group of physicians who helped future mothers practice natural birth. This didn't mean that these physicians would not use medical interventions such as C-section, Pitocin induction of labor, or episiotomy if they deemed it necessary. When I spoke to them, they were curious to find out how I saw birth and accepted it as a possibility rather than an unusual and burdensome desire on my part.

Looking back on my experience, I feel very fortunate that I found this particular group practice. Throughout my pregnancy I felt supported in my desire to complete a natural birth. For example, my doctors constantly reminded me about the wisdom of my body. They took time to educate me about the different changes that my body was going through and were careful to normalize the process. While it might seem trivial to a provider who sees several pregnant women a day, it was reassuring to hear different stories about women who shared similar experiences. After each visit, I felt confident about my body and myself.

My physicians also provided me with information about the benefits of prenatal yoga. Doing yoga made me contemplate my abilities, taught me how to access more of them, connected me with like-minded expectant mothers, and most of all, assured me that my practitioner truly considered the wisdom of my body.

Most importantly, during the labor, my physician followed my lead and we experienced the birthing process as I had envisioned it. Even though I was attached to an IV, I was able to walk around the hospital unit, sit in a chair, dance with my partner, and finally give birth in a variety of birthing positions, rather than just lying flat on my back. My physician was a true team player; he believed in my abilities, gave me opportunities, and provided needed support to reach my goal.

My Doula

A few months into my pregnancy, I started to look for birthing classes. I already knew that I would be giving birth in a hospital, so I first looked for what was available in that hospital. I did find a schedule of classes provided by the hospital, but was not convinced that they were in line with my philosophy of birthing. I decided to look for a practitioner who could help me with hypnosis training specifically for the birth process. At that time I was already a certified hypnotherapist, but I had much to learn about the application of hypnosis to the birthing process. I usually worked on pain management with my clients, and I thought that birthing pain would be different from, for instance, the back pain after a tennis match. Only later did I learn that many research studies had demonstrated that mothers had a greater satisfaction with their childbirth and fewer medical interventions when they utilized a doula (Simkin 2008). As explained by DONA International, the professional doula association, the term doula refers to an experienced and trained professional who provides physical, emotional, and spiritual support before, during, and just after birth. Translated literally from Greek, the word doula means "a woman who serves." In practice, doulas' services can range from providing a calm and warm presence to giving a light massage, to facilitating hypnotic techniques, or serving as an intermediary between the woman in labor and medical practitioners. A doula is there to explain physiological changes associated with the birthing process, provide emotional support to the woman's partner, and reassure the family about the mother's feelings and sensations.

That search led me to Diana, a doula trained in the Mongan method of HypnoBirthing. Reflecting back on my experience, I'm struck by the paucity of information available about doula-related services, hypnosis-related providers, and about how to make an educated choice among these practitioners. The two worlds of hospitals and birthing centers seemed disconnected, making it difficult for expectant mothers to build a bridge between them. As a consumer, it's like having to shop for clothes that are still covered by thick plastic bags.

I had the good fortune to find a doula who was also a Hypnobirthing Practitioner. I participated in a class of five lectures, which I attended with my husband and another couple who were planning a natural birth. The class introduced us to Mongan's method, instructed us to read the book, listen to the CD, and practice our breathing. Our partners were also educated about natural birth and taught how to assist the birthing mother during labor. We explored our wishes about the birth and shared with each other our fears, hopes, and desires for our future child. We also watched videos of natural delivery with and without Mongan's method. Most of all, these videos and classes were helpful for my husband, who had expected to see women screaming in pain, but instead saw calm women in the process of birthing their beloved child. Tension replaced pain and waves replaced contractions. The HypnoBirthing classes allowed us to see the birthing process from an entirely new perspective.

The doula was helpful in a way that I had not expected. When my water broke and I called my doula, I found out that just a few hours before, her other client's water broke and she was giving birth in the same hospital a few rooms down from me. That is why I found myself with another doula assisting me during the birthing process, a doula unfamiliar with hypnobirth.

It was clear from the first moment that this new doula was treating me exactly as she would any other expecting mother. Assuming that I was in pain, she offered to give me a massage, to rub my feet, and to bring me ice chips. The ice was helpful. I was starving, because in the hospital giving birth, I was not allowed to eat! Despite her obvious difficulty relating to my expectations, I appreciated the doula's assistance: her calm presence, her availability, and her willingness to assist were assets in a hospital where otherwise I would have to depend on the help of busy nurses. The highlight of my experience of this doula was her comment just after I gave birth. As I was holding my daughter in my arms, the doula approached me and exclaimed, "I learned so much during this birth. I have never witnessed anything like this. I would like to learn how to use hypnosis during birth; it will change the birthing experience of my future clients."

My Partner

I cannot imagine my birth without my husband's presence. It is easy to forget that not so long ago, fathers were excluded from the birthing scene. The big shift happened in the 1970s, when, following Lamaze's teaching, fathers started to replace doulas to comfort and support expecting mothers (England 1998). Since that time, the role of the father was quickly established, and today mothers' partners have many opportunities to be involved in the birth in a variety of contexts.

Despite the fact that multiple authors discuss the partner's role during birth (England and Horowitz 1998; Simkin 2008), before I gave birth my obstetricians did not prepare or even talk to my husband about his role. It is possible that the doctor assumed my partner already knew about it from somewhere else. However, thinking back, it seems a strange assumption that my husband would know what to do during the birthing process. It is possible that our obstetrician did not discuss the event with my husband because we were planning to have a doula during labor. However, it is important for any obstetrics practice to have a process in place to ensure that critical information is delivered to the partner as well as the expectant mother.

Addressing the dos and don'ts of a partner attending labor, England and Horowitz (1998) provide several key recommendations to the mother and the partner:

- Be Yourself: the partner is encouraged not to take on any specific role, but to behave as usual and relate to the birthing mother in a natural way.
- The partner is encouraged to become a guardian of the birthplace: when I was in labor, a nurse came several times and asked me if I was in pain. Instructed in the importance of language, my husband finally stated: "Please do not use that word around my wife. She is not in pain."

- Partners are encouraged to protect the birthing mother's privacy: "Like other mammals, human mothers may unconsciously or instinctively inhibit their labor or birth in a situation that feels unfamiliar, if not unsafe" (England and Horowitz 1998, 169). For different women, this might mean different things, because all of us have different standards for privacy. For some it might involve dimmed lights, for others being able to change into a clean birthing gown when desired, while for others it might mean having the least number of people in the room as possible.
- Partners are encouraged to offer realistic support: while my husband could not experience what I was experiencing, holding his hand and listening to him read a text that we had chosen together previously helped me relax and concentrate on my childbirth.

England and Horowitz (1998) also encourage husbands to take care of themselves. While birthing mothers function under the interactions of multiple hormones, fathers and other partners do not have this luxury. Thus, they should be reminded to eat, drink, and have some rest in order to remain the most helpful for a birthing mother.

Other Helpers

When my water broke, I was at home. I called my doula, my doctor in the hospital, and, after eating a large breakfast, I went to the hospital. My parents, who had traveled from Russia to assist me during birth, and my husband accompanied me. My mom was new to the concept of my husband being with me during the birth. In Russia, my father was not even allowed on the hospital floor, let alone to assist during labor. If asked, my father could not describe what a man would do during birth. And of course, my parents had not been with us when we were preparing for birth during our Hypnobirthing classes, nor did they know much about hypnosis or doulas. They just wanted to help.

When we arrived, I let my parents come to the room to sit a little bit with me, and then I actually asked them to go home. While I love them dearly, there was just not enough room for so many people, and I felt observed rather than helped. As England and Horowitz (1998) put it, "Ask this person to come not because you think she or he would like to be there, but because you *want* her or him here" (13). In this case, I already knew whom I wanted to be present during my birth, the roles had been given and rehearsed, and additional people felt out of place.

Reflecting one more time on the process of creating my birthing team, I am aware of the disconnection between the different healthcare providers involved in the process. I was the only connection between the obstetrician, the doula, and my husband. No efforts were made to coordinate roles, create a common treatment plan, or provide psychoeducation. If I had not been so involved in my birthing process, I would have felt that disconnection. It is important for healthcare providers to consider who should take the initiative and how to develop a collaborative effort during the birthing process so that each person in the team works together to achieve the safest, most comfortable birth possible, whether in a hospital, birthing center, or at home.

FIVE

Hypnotic Essentials

A hypnotic experience is constructed from a combination of sensations, feelings, and memories. A familiar smell might bring a vivid association, a particular word might establish a new helpful connection, and a breathing pattern might allow relating in a new way to a familiar situation. All these different elements might be considered as part of hypnotic essentials utilized by a person to experience and benefit from trance. Finding out what brings peace and comfort to the expectant mother and learning to utilize breathing constitute the first steps towards achieving your goals while utilizing hypnosis during pregnancy and delivery.

FINDING YOUR ELEMENT

One of my fondest memories from my pregnancy is going for a swim in the pool every morning. Each person has an element in which one feels the most comfortable. By element, I mean a tangible or intangible environment: a place, a memory, a sound, a smell, a touch, a shape, a color that brings the most comfort when we picture it or imagine ourselves in it. Stop for a moment to picture your element. I purposefully did not use the word "think," because our element is part of our sensory experience, something that comes naturally to mind as the first option among many others. In fact, it does not have to be something unique or static; it might be a series of things, or something that differs for different activities. Our personal elements represent something we can access any time we need to concentrate or relax.

Anne Morrow Lindbergh (2005) speaks lovingly about her restorative element in her book *Gift from the Sea*, in which she describes her yearly trips to the beach. She writes:

> Rollers on the beach, wind in the pines, the slow flapping of herons
> across sand dunes, drown out the hectic rhythms of city and suburb,
> time tables, and schedules. One falls under their spell, relaxes, stretches
> out prone. One becomes, in fact, like the element on which one lies,
> flattened by the sea; bare, open, empty as the beach, erased by today's
> tides of all yesterday's scribblings. (10)

One can almost feel how that element relaxes her body and allows it
to be replenished. However, while some find the beach relaxing and the
ocean peaceful, others may experience the same environment as draining
and anxiety provoking, but find snowfall relaxing. We should all restless-
ly search to identify our own element, without compromising or expecting a universality of experience.

Water has always been my personal element. I relate to it on many
levels. I fondly recall my father teaching me to swim. I love my father
dearly and as a child always enjoyed spending time with him. He taught
me that that water will hold me if I just trust the current and let it support
my body. I can still hear his voice saying, "You don't need to do anything. Just lie on the water and rest." Being in the water meant being free
and supported. It meant trust. When I grew older, I learned to appreciate
the beauty of the water, so that being near the water was as relaxing as
being in it. I could spend hours watching the waves or smelling the sea.
With each breath of the ocean, I could feel myself getting calmer, re-
stored, and hopeful.

When I became pregnant, water remained my favorite element. With
my growing belly, I felt clumsy when I was walking or running. In the
water, the weight was lifted, and I again felt graceful. After spending at
least fifteen minutes swimming, I felt rejuvenated and soon it became my
daily routine. Swimming not only relaxed my body, it also gave me an
opportunity to think and center my attention on my connection with my
growing baby. I would talk to my daughter, wondering what she felt
while I was moving in the water, relaxed and content. I wondered if she
would develop her own special connection with the water, finding it as
calming and restorative as I do.

My time in the water also allowed me to practice my breathing exercises. I knew I had to practice my breathing throughout my pregnancy to
be able to use it purposefully during the birth. I also knew that I would
need to develop a specific routine to make the practice diligent, making
sure to engage in each type of breathing regularly. The practice also
brought me a sense of peacefulness: exercises helped me to develop an
appreciation for taking one moment at a time, sometimes allowing myself
to embrace timelessness and savor the moment. This time also gave me
the opportunity to think about my future birth. I would frequently imagine using my breathing techniques, feeling my body transform, and
meeting my daughter for the first time. Memories, wishes, and sensations
would blend together during these memorable moments.

I knew from the beginning of my pregnancy that I wanted to give birth in a hospital. As much as I liked the idea of giving birth in the water, it was not possible for me, as the hospital in my area was not equipped for such a delivery. Still, I wanted to bring the peacefulness of my morning breathing environment with me to the hospital. Since I was not able to be in the water physically, I decided to bring the memory of being in the water. Each day I paid particular attention to the sensations I experienced while creating mental images of my element. I was mindful to notice the reflections of the sun in the water or the flight of a seagull above me. Eventually, I was able to recreate the environment of my element through these images, smells, and sensations no matter where I was; keeping these pictures in my mind had the same effect as actually experiencing those events firsthand. I found that I brought my water with me wherever I went.

Engage your patient, the future mother, in thinking about her element. After you discover the element that makes her feel comfortable, you can use her connection with it in the different ways I described above, as well as in new ways that make sense for her. Here are a few simple tips that might help you engage your patients in a conversation about their favorite element:

- Remember that different people experience comfort and relaxation very differently. What is relaxing for one person may not be relaxing for another.
- The expectant mother's element might be constant throughout her life and then change during pregnancy, or even during the time of birth. Encourage her not to be attached to a particular element, but to pay attention to her sensations and what feels comfortable in the moment. For example, for a long time I felt very comfortable in a forest among tall trees, listening to the wind rustling through the foliage, awakening to the sounds of birds, and finding relaxation in the colors of the woods. However, as time passed, my association with the forest started to evoke a distinct time for reading, writing, and creating. This image, while still relaxing, did not resonate with me during my pregnancy — probably because it did not involve my physical sensations, which were more prominent when I was immersed in water. I did not try to talk myself into staying with the image of the forest, but instead embraced what felt the most natural at that moment in time.
- The element does not have to evoke or be something that actually happened or is happening. For some women, creating their own image or world is more soothing and beneficial. Others might remember a sensation from the past. I once attended a workshop by well-known psychotherapist Yvonne Dolan. She spoke about a friend who had asked her to help him overcome his fear of flying.

Yvonne helped him recreate an image of a very comfortable chair he had once owned. Imagining himself sitting in that chair, Yvonne's friend felt instantly more relaxed and was able to focus less on his fear of flying. Even though the chair was old and had had to be replaced, his mental image of it was more comforting than the actual chair.

- Encourage your patients to curiously explore their element by paying attention to each specific detail. They can also find ways to compare themselves to a particular element. For example, my mother shared with me that when she was giving birth, she noticed a tree outside that was swaying under the pressure of the wind. She compared her own body to the swaying tree, so each time she felt contractions, she breathed and moved forward with her body like the tree.
- The more your patients interact with their element, the more familiar they become with it. They then can use this familiarity and the details they conjure in their mind to create their place of comfort. In fact, concentrating on these details and becoming curious about them eventually distracts them from their fears, anxiety, or discomfort.
- Progressive relaxation can help your patients become curious about the sensations in their bodies, examining them part by part, noticing where they feel the most tension and the most relaxation, and watching how these sensations change while they examine them.
- Remember that your patients don't have to have a constant element or stick to only one. They can also explore the surrounding environment, or be captured by certain characteristics of their present experience, and be able to recreate a relaxing or comfortable sensation on the spot.
- Finally, remind your patients that they don't have to make these explorations alone. You can help them find their way or refer them to a qualified hypnotherapist before they continue practicing on their own.

I BREATHE, THEREFORE I AM

Breathing is essential to our existence. While it is clear that one has to inhale and exhale in order to remain alive, breathing is much more than simply our need for air. In fact, breathing is a powerful tool in many practices, including mindfulness, meditation, and hypnosis. In these instances, instead of being an unconscious activity, breathing becomes a conscious, specific practice in which the person is engaging. Breathing exercises include different ways to become aware of our breathing mechanisms and environment, as well as ways to establish specific breathing patterns with a specific purpose.

To achieve mindfulness, we are simply invited to refocus our attention on our breathing. As explained by Kabat-Zinn (2005), "Bringing awareness to our breathing, we remind ourselves that we are here now, so we might as well be fully awake for whatever is already happening" (18). Sometimes in the midst of a hectic schedule, when I feel like I cannot find time to "catch my breath," I remind myself to experience a moment of stillness. I stop everything I am doing and take a deep breath in and out and remember the purpose of whatever activity I am doing. That helps me see the larger picture of my involvement without getting lost in details. The same is true during a heated argument, when taking a deep breath means refocusing on my own sensations and seeing the situation from an outsider's perspective.

Breathing can be used in hypnosis to induce trance and to get in sync with the multiple sensations experienced by our bodies and our minds. In this case, breathing becomes an important part of a specific activity through a specific breathing pattern that amplifies certain physical actions and concentrates our mind on a particular activity. During birth, breathing becomes a synonym for birthing. If we conceptualize the birthing process as different stages of physical changes, such as the thinning and opening of the uterus stage or the active birthing stage, we can also pinpoint specific breathing exercises that can help the woman concentrate on a specific way of relating to her body and to her baby.

As described previously, Marie Mongan (2005) was particularly skillful in describing different breathing patterns. In *HypnoBirthing*, she distinguishes three distinct breathing patterns: sleep breathing, slow breathing, and birth breathing. Mongan assigns a particular function to each of these patterns and provides specific exercises that help the woman gain ease before the actual childbirth. In that way, during the birth, the breathing exercises can be a seamless practice rather than a conscious effort. Mongan recommends a regular practice of all these techniques starting early in pregnancy.

Sleep Breathing

The main purpose of the sleep breathing exercises is relaxation. When experiencing contractions (called "surges" in HypnoBirthing), women tend to stiffen and become rigid. This is a natural reaction to an unusual sensation. However, it is usually counterproductive. As described by Ina Gaskin (2003), the excretory and the reproductive sphincters function best in a relaxed atmosphere of familiarity and privacy. Therefore, anything that can relax the birthing mother is helpful in that process. At the same time, relaxed women can also take advantage of such hypnosis-related techniques as visualization and imagery. The relaxed body also can replenish itself with energy for the second stage of labor, when the child is actually being born.

To achieve sleep breathing, Mongan (2005) describes the following technique:

> Draw in a breath from your stomach. To a count of four, mentally recite "In 1–2–3–4"on the intake. Feel your stomach rise as you draw the breath up and into the back of your throat. As you exhale, mentally recite "Out 1–2–3–4–5–6–7–8." Do not exhale through your mouth. As you breath out very slowly through your nose, direct the energy of the breath down and inward toward the back of your throat, allowing your shoulders to droop into the frame of your body. (125)

To ensure that the birthing mother is executing the technique correctly, Mongan continues, "place your left hand on your stomach and your right hand on the lower part of your chest. As you inhale, you should feel your left hand rising as though your stomach were inflating like a balloon. As you exhale, you will feel your hands fold into each other, as your chest and stomach create a crevice" (Mongan 2005, 125).

Slow Breathing

By performing slow breathing during the thinning and opening of the uterus stage, women can facilitate the opening of sphincters by amplifying the upward movement of the uterus. If we compare the uterus to a balloon filling with air, we can say that by engaging in this type of breathing, women work along with their birthing organ by engaging in specific breathing patterns.

To practice this technique, Mongan (2005) gives women the following instructions:

> Lying in a lateral position, place your hands across the top of your abdomen so that your fingers barely meet. Exhale briefly to clear your lungs and nasal passages. Slowly and gradually draw in your breath to a rapid count from 1 to 20+ as though you were inflating your belly. *Avoid using short intakes of breath* [emphasis the author's]; it can tire you and requires that you take several breaths in order to get through the surge. The slow intake to a rapid count up to 20+ and the equally slow exhalation will allow you sufficient time to work with each surge. If it is necessary for you to take a second breath during a surge, do so in the very same manner. Do not hold your breath — ever. . . . While breathing in, focus your attention on your rising abdomen and bring the surge up as much as you can; visualize filling a balloon inside your abdomen as you draw in. *Slowly* exhale to the same count, breathing downward and outward. (127)

Ina Gaskin (2003) also mentions the slow breathing, emphasizing its importance to other organs, such as the heart, nervous system, and lungs. "Besides that, it gives [women's] abdominal organs a gentle massage, increases the wavelike squeezing movements of [women's] intestines, and strengthens the blood circulation in [women's] abdominal organs to help them function properly" (177).

Birth Breathing

This type of breathing is used during the second stage of labor. Movies about childbirth often show nurses instructing mothers to push as hard as they can to give birth. Mongan (2005) argues that such pushing is actually counterproductive, as it contributes to the closure of the reproductive sphincter, damages muscles of the pelvic floor, and contributes to the woman's exhaustion. By engaging in birth breathing, women gradually move the baby down while the sphincter remains open.

Like the previous techniques, Mongan recommends that the woman practice birth breathing daily. She (2005) instructs that the best way to practice is sitting on a toilet while having a bowel movement and taking short in-breaths while becoming aware of the gently nudging breath and body pulsations. Mongan instructs,

> Close your eyes to avoid tearing the blood vessels in your eyes. Placing the tip of your tongue at the place where your front teeth and palate meet will help your lower jaw to recede so that you remain free of tension in your mouth and jaw area. This also helps relax the vagina outlet. When you feel the onset of a surge, follow it. Take a short, but deep, breath through your nose and direct the energy of that breath to the lower back of your throat and down through your body behind your baby in the form of a "J"—down and forward. Allow the muscles in your vaginal area to open as though you were letting the breath out through them or moving your bowels. Don't ride out or hang on to a breath beyond its effectiveness and don't allow those lower muscles to tighten. Repeat this process to take in another short, deep breath and breathe down in the same pattern as above—and then another. (130)

Utilizing breathing techniques in these different situations gives the birthing mother an opportunity to connect with her body, avoid automatic reactions produced by her body, achieve a relaxed state of mind necessary to concentrate on the birthing sensations, and provide a safe and successful birth. Practicing the breathing pattern allows the future mother to get in sync with her body long before the actual birth, making the breathing her natural connection to her body and her mind.

SIX

Hypnotic Aids

Even though hypnosis can be seen as a number of techniques that use the person's suggestibility to induce a trance-like state, the effectiveness of hypnosis lies in the ability to evoke the required state as needed, and thus, in the person's ability to evoke certain experiences through hypnotic intervention or self-hypnosis. Therefore, the use of hypnosis during birth is most beneficial when certain aspects of the hypnotic philosophy have been integrated in the woman's daily routine and are an inseparable part of the expectant mother's life style. These aspects include the ability to explore unknown sensations with curiosity, the ability to use developed coping strategies to face unpleasant circumstances, the ability to trust imagination as a guiding compass for further exploration. The hypnotic philosophy is built through practice, with the learned behaviors and techniques ultimately becoming a way of being.

As has been discussed, healthcare professionals play a vital role in helping women get ready for the birth day by providing them with important information about hypnotic techniques and the development of specific skills that can help the women before, during, and after the delivery. This chapter describes three hypnotic approaches — visualization, yoga, and music. Their effectiveness is supported by contemporary research. You can offer these to your clients as potential aids during their pregnancy and childbirth.

VISUALIZATION

Visualization helps a client envision her desired outcome. Several studies found visualization helpful in many circumstances. In fact, the mental training that allows us to imagine an event without actually performing it has been investigated and proved to be beneficial during pregnancy, birth, and postpartum (Hildingsson 2012). Nabb, Kimber, Haines, and McCourt (2006) also researched the effects of visualization, along with other complementary therapies, and found it beneficial for changing women's perception of pain during labor.

Visualization rests on basic Ericksonian techniques, such as implication and presupposition, to induce trance. As described by O'Hanlon and Martin (1992), "probably the simplest way to understand implication and presupposition is to imagine that there is something that is going to happen or is happening or did happen" (16). For example, you can imply that the expectant mother is going to have a satisfying birth. The goals can be determined with the patient by using the Miracle Question, while helping your patient to create an ideal vision of her birth.

To help your patient visualize the goal, you have to "speak as if that goal is absolutely going to happen and then you can speculate within that certainty how that goal is going to be attained" (O'Hanlon and Martin 1992, 16). For example, a successful birth might look different for different women. It is important to assess the specific understanding of a successful birth in order to help the expectant mother create an image in as much detail as possible. Providing enough details also gives room for any variation in the actual experience, without its feeling like a failure and unaccomplished dream. In a sense, an attitude of equifinality, that is, the systems-based concept that different paths are different means to reach the same outcome, can reassure future mothers that unusual circumstances and unexpected feelings ultimately will be part of their overall experience of a successful birth.

Shakti Gawain (2002), the author of *Creative Visualization Workbook*, writes that the "imagination is the ability to create an idea, a mental picture, or a feeling sense of something" (4). We repeat the act of visualization by using affirmation, stories, or metaphors. In fact, Gawain cautions readers not to think of visualization as only a visual activity. She invites people to use whichever sense is most useful, forthcoming, and comfortable to the individual. Gawain instructs, "it is not at all necessary to mentally see an image" (18). Rather we can sense, smell, hear, or see an image that we choose to create.

The expectant mother can also choose to concentrate on a specific aspect of the birthing process. For instance, some women associate successful birth with progressing smoothly with their opening of the cervix during the first stage of labor. In that case, you can provide the expectant mother with enough details about the anatomy to help her to create the images needed to visualize that goal. One of the visualization techniques that Marie Mongan (2005) provided in *HypnoBirthing* and that I personally found helpful is called the "opening blossom" exercise. In this visualization, the cervix is viewed as an opening flower. During the preparatory class, participants are encouraged to envision the flower opening petal by petal. I actually drew my own representation of the flower, tried to feel its texture and sense its smell. I then spent time visualizing the flower opening even before I was in actual labor. I also used that technique during my active labor and found it extremely helpful.

It is important to emphasize that the woman's expectation should not be to achieve a *specific* outcome by using this technique. Should the mother expect that this technique would bring specific "positive" outcomes, failure to advance in that particular way will bring more frustration than benefit. Therefore, these techniques should be presented as ways of moving toward the desired goal, without certainty about which step will be the most beneficial one. The important point is to take the next step with confidence, almost as if the expectant mother were climbing a mountain and enjoying the trip, just as she would enjoy reaching the peak of the mountain.

Another distinction to make is that between visualization and guided imagery. While both techniques can be effective to induce trance, the difference between the two lies in the directness of the method of delivery. Visualization has fewer directives, with the caregiver providing minimal information to orient the client's experience. This gives her the freedom to create and recreate images, based on her experiences and current sensations. For example, if an image of a flower had been suggested to me, I could have come up with a different image or could have imagined a flower of a specific shape and form that was meaningful to me.

Guided imagery, on the other hand, is more directive. Usually the woman is led through the imagery with specific directions via a script and/or CD to produce a certain effect (for example, relaxation). Although several studies on the beneficial effect of the guided imagery (Jallo, Cozens, Smith, and Simpson 2013; Gedde-Dahl and Fors 2012) have found that it can be easily implemented by a person with minimum training in hypnosis, I have reservations. In my view, each person needs individualized guidance, especially when the situation is potentially anxiety provoking, such as childbirth. A personalized approach helps the healthcare provider ensure that the technique is beneficial and not causing any harm to the patient. One example from my HypnoBirthing classes illustrates my concern.

The first part of the class was dedicated to the ability of women's bodies to naturally adjust in order to birth a child. The second part of the class was designed for the women to experience a variety of techniques that we could potentially use when in labor. One evening all the participants, including the women's partners, were invited to experience guided imagery. The teacher told us to close our eyes and then proceeded to read a script. In the script, we were invited to explore a house (real or imaginary), go to its kitchen, and there, envision a knife and a lemon. We were instructed to take the knife and cut the citrus in two halves. We were guided to experience the sour sensation in our mouths as if we had actually eaten the lemon.

Not only did I not see anything distinctive to our needs in that script, but also I found that being pregnant, sitting in an unfamiliar place, and visualizing a knife created uneasiness. When I asked my husband what he had experienced, he stated that he also was particularly anxious after the session. It took some debriefing with each other and with the teacher to get past that feeling.

If you choose to use or suggest a specific script for guided imagery, reassure your patient that she can adjust it as needed in her imagination. It is also important afterward to take some time for debriefing, exploring what her reactions were to the script. Most importantly, become and remain curious about your patient's experiences and be ready to alter the script or to use a different one more appropriate for your patient's sensibilities.

To summarize, both techniques of visualization and guided imagery need to be practiced often and as far in advance as possible. By encouraging your patients to regularly engage in these practices, responding to implication and presupposition will become second nature to them, no matter what the technique, even during the most powerful experience of their lives, the birth of their child.

YOGA

According to Narendran, Nagarathna, Narendran, Gunasheela, and Nagendra (2005), "The word yoga comes from the Sanskrit root *yuj* that means to yoke, to join, and to direct and concentrate one's attention. The practice was first described by Patanjali in his classic work *Yoga Sutras*" (242). It is built on three main pillars: deep bodily relaxation achieved in different postures (called *asanas*), decreased respiratory rate via controlled slow breathing (called *pranayama*), and mental steadiness reached by techniques such as meditation and chanting.

The practice of yoga has been documented to have positive effects on both men and on women whether they are pregnant or not. While there is still room for further investigation, a preliminary research study demonstrates such benefits of a regular practice of yoga as lowered respiratory rate through slow, controlled breathing and relaxation through meditation and chanting (Sun, Hung, Chung, and Kuo 2010).

Recently yoga has been investigated to determine if it has specific benefits for pregnant women. Prenatal yoga practice was found to have several positive effects, including a greater awareness of inner sensations and emotions and increased coping strategies for childbirth. The slow, diaphragmatic breathing of yoga helps the expectant mother relax and initiate coping strategies during the first and second stage of labor. In addition, these help her respond to perceived pain with less stress and greater calm, leading to more rapid recovery from stress and greater capacity to concentrate on her labor and specific techniques that help during the birthing stage (Sun et al. 2010). The practice of yoga also has specific benefits on the health of the fetus and has been demonstrated to increase the mean gestational age of babies (Nabb, Kimbler, Haines, and McCourt 2006).

Overall, a regular practice of yoga not only reduces discomfort during pregnancy and boosts women's self-confidence about the childbirth, but also teaches women about the different abilities of their bodies, including the innate capacity to give birth (Sun et al. 2010). Yoga sets a tone and habit of self-care before and during the childbirth by encouraging an inner and outer balance achieved through self-awareness.

When comparing yoga's effects with hypnosis, Yapko (1995) noted psychological and physiological characteristics of a hypnotic state that are similar to the goal of yoga, in which people experience a change in breathing rate (usually slower, but an increasing rate is also possible), change in pulse rate (usually slower), and muscle relaxation. For example, most people associate hypnosis with an experience of relaxation. Mind and body become more susceptible to invitations to complete specific actions and follow certain trains of thoughts (that also can be positively utilized during the birthing process). That is why most individuals follow through on a hypnotherapist's suggestions. We can see how yoga philosophy and exercise can be beneficial for expectant mothers and can enhance their experience of hypnosis, if they choose to incorporate this method as part of their birthing process.

While yoga originated as an aspect of Hinduism, the practice of yoga does not require acceptance of religious beliefs or philosophy. Rather, "the goal of this ancient tradition [is] to calm the restless mind and seamlessly unite the mind, body, and spirit, to promote positive health, self-awareness and spirituality" (Narendran et al. 2003, 242). Like hypnosis, yoga transcends its philosophical and theoretical framework and can be adapted to fit each person's needs. In fact, many yoga techniques are used in birthing classes, usually when the focus is on the importance of the breath. Besides exercises such as walking and swimming, some yoga postures also have been discovered to be beneficial (Mongan 2005).

A significant, sometimes overwhelming, variety of yoga classes are available in most locations. To help an expectant mother sort through the possibilities and find the best teacher for her, it is important for health-care professionals to offer a referral list of prenatal yoga teachers to their patients who are interested. This will demonstrate to your clients the value you attribute to prenatal yoga as a type of self-care, which may increase the likelihood of the mother's follow-through with your recommendation. In addition, such referrals might increase the quality of the yoga teacher chosen. Remember to recommend only *prenatal* yoga. Regular yoga classes might do more harm than good for expectant mothers.

After making the referral, providers need to learn if their patient wants to follow up on the recommendation. Her decision itself will be important information for you. If the woman decides not to attempt yoga, the provider can learn more by asking such questions as

- What has stopped you from making the contact?
- What other relaxation techniques are you planning to use while approaching birth?
- What exercises have you been practicing and what sensations have you been experiencing as a result?

If the future mother decides to try prenatal yoga, it is important that you ask about her experience once she has started. Classes vary greatly, and the woman might attribute problematic aspects of the class to yoga in general, when it may be the idiosyncratic feature of that particular yoga class or teacher.

For example, I had a negative and positive experience with yoga during my pregnancy. I had been looking for a yoga teacher because I thought the philosophy was in line with my interest in a natural birth with the assistance of hypnosis. I had found some information in the leaflets in the waiting room of my OBGYN and decided to explore the classes. My first experience was quite positive. I liked the postures that we practiced, because I found them relaxing and stimulating at the same time. I also felt connected to the teacher and liked sharing the experience with other pregnant women in the classes.

Mongan (2005) encourages expectant mothers to surround themselves with positive stories about childbirth. My positive experience of the prenatal yoga classes changed when a different instructor took over. The new teacher started the class by informing us that she viewed yoga class not only as an exercise for pregnant women, but also as a support group for them. Unfortunately, such reframing changed the dynamic of the group, inviting mothers to share experiences that I could not relate to at that time. While this may have been helpful to other attendees, it prevented me from focusing on my own sensations and experiences and remaining positive after the exercise. Ultimately, I decided to stop attending the class. This experience illustrates that what is important for some expectant mothers might not be a good fit for others; thus, it is important to let the expectant mothers know that the format and structure of yoga classes may vary depending on the instructors.

It is vital that, besides trusting their yoga instructor, your patients also listen to their own body. Especially during pregnancy, their body is often very much in tune with their needs. I learned that lesson one day after an exercise in my yoga class. When I went home, my body felt very sore. I talked to another woman in the same class, and she had actually gone to the ER that afternoon after the class. For many women, it is difficult to ignore the instructions, no matter how unwise they may be. So remind your patients to stay mindful of and trust their own sensations and reactions to each exercise, asking their yoga instructor any questions as needed. In collaboration, you are setting up yourself and your patient for the most personalized and beneficial exercise and relaxation plan to benefit the expectant mother now and in the future.

MUSIC

Have you ever been so moved by a musical piece that you forgot where you were, why you were there, and how you got there? It could have been a relaxing or moving melody or an intense concerto, or a gentle lullaby. If we hear a piece of music that fits with our experience at the right moment, we can feel as if we have become one with music. Many of us have experienced this kind of an informal trance.

This response to music can be used during childbirth, providing expectant mothers a means to relax, manage their anxiety, and cope with their pain. In fact, Browning (2000) notes that music, especially rhythm, has the capacity to induce certain physical and emotional responses in the brain and body. By conditioning a certain response to a specifically chosen melody, music can also help women develop particular coping strategies in advance of childbirth.

There are several ways to use music in these situations. If the expectant mother has selected specific images to use during labor, she can choose certain songs or music to go with them. Also, music can be used to mirror the mother's sensations, adding to her experience of her feelings. For example, the volume of the music can be increased to match intensifying contractions during the first stage of labor. Instead of the caregiver trying to calm the mother, the volume of the music provides her a way to join with her sensations. As the music becomes part of other sensations (joy, anger, and so on) she is experiencing, the mother in labor is no longer focused on one sensation, but can diffuse her attention among multiple experiences, giving her relief. This technique draws on the concept of boundary discussed by Gregory Bateson (2000). He stated that as long as we focus on differences, we heighten them. On the other hand, if we see similarities or embrace a multitude of sensations without feeling the need to define them, we can enter a different relationship with our body and our mind.

Additionally, different melodies can ease sensations by modifying the birthing environment. For example, future mothers can use sounds that reflect the ideal environment they had already envisioned for their childbirth. England and Horowitz (1998) cite research indicating that sounds of nature positively influence mothers in labor by increasing relaxation.

They suggest listening to the sounds in the outside world, such as sounds of the rain, singing birds, and so on, during pregnancy and then using recordings of sounds of nature (for example, ocean waves, wind in the forest, and so on) when confined to the indoor environment of a hospital or birthing center.

Finally, music can stimulate certain sensations or behaviors by introducing a different rhythm to the birthing process. For example, if the laboring mother is feeling tired, an invigorating tempo can stimulate further activity in the progression of labor. On the other side, if the woman is upset, relaxing music is a nice addition to her coping techniques.

Remember the Ericksonian principle of utilization (Haley 1993). It is important to recognize that adjectives such as "calming," "relaxing," and "energizing" are relative. Each woman has her own definition of what constitutes relaxation to her. What might sound calming and soothing to one person might evoke the opposite reaction in another. When I was working in a nursing home, I often spoke to the music therapist about his work. He recognized that similar types of music have different effects on different people. To build a repertoire for an individual, the music therapist would talk to the nursing home residents (if they could not talk, he would solicit ideas from their relatives). He would then play a few pieces to see the person's verbal and nonverbal responses, and based on that information, he would choose a few songs that he would regularly play for that person.

A similar approach is recommended for expectant mothers. Browning (2000) encourages expectant mothers to select several musical pieces that are particularly relaxing or energizing for them and to make their recording of the music and listen to it frequently to create the conditioned response to the music.

In my own pregnancy, my doula advised me to prepare and listen to my own tape of music I had chosen. I was very glad I did. Although I usually appreciated classical music, I did not find it relaxing when I was pregnant. When envisioning my birthing process, I was more attracted to rhythmic, techno music. In fact, my favorite melody of that time was *Stereo Love* by Edward Maya and Vika Jigulina. Since this song existed in different versions, I created a tape of the various arrangements of the same song. I ended up spending most of my twelve-hour labor listening to that tape.

By listening to the selected music regularly, the expectant mother can create specific rituals to accompany the childbirth. For example, several themes can be established in advance, such as "my lullaby," "my relaxation," and "my concentration." These musical themes will help the mother attend to her various needs during the delivery and can orient her birthing partner to the different needs of the future mother, giving him or her an opportunity to participate in the birthing process when it will be difficult to ask the laboring woman to explain her wishes. The chosen piece of music can help to translate her desires to her birthing partner without requiring a lengthy explanation.

Several authors point out the influence of music on the unborn baby, its reaction to music heard while in utero, and its increased ability to calm while listening to the music after being born (Arya, Chansoria, Konanki, and Tiwari 2012; Poreba, Dudkiewicz, and Drygalski 2000). Using music in this way, mothers can start building this relationship with their unborn child, which will make the childbirth process a long-awaited encounter rather than merely necessary discomfort and anxiety to endure, unrelated to the act of the birth of the baby.

Although music can be helpful in the ways above, it is important to remember that the mother's sensations and perceptions might change during the actual labor. What sounded calming in a relaxed home atmosphere might be annoying in a hospital environment during the actual birth. Therefore, as with any other technique, it is crucial to instruct the expectant mother to be aware of her emotions and to change the music as needed. In addition, encourage the people supporting the woman during the labor process to notice her verbal and nonverbal cues that indicate her comfort with specific music. This potential change in perception is another reason that a variety of melodies should be chosen before the birthing process.

The healthcare provider needs to endorse the use of music, especially if the woman plans to give birth in a hospital. Expectant mothers might be hesitant to ask about using music in the unfamiliar environment of a hospital. It is the job of the physicians or other helping professionals at the birthing site to encourage the mother to use this coping strategy. She also should be instructed that she might need to use headsets in a hospital environment to avoid disturbing other expectant mothers and nurses who take care of them.

To conclude, the use of music can be combined with other techniques such as deep breathing and visualization, discussed earlier. No techniques should be considered in isolation, but rather as pieces of a mosaic that provide a supportive environment in preparation for the birth and during the birthing process.

SEVEN

Hypnobirth in Action

It is not enough for your patients to learn about hypnotic techniques; they also have to learn how to apply them. It is quite difficult to rehearse the birthing, since each situation will be unique, requiring a specific skill set. However, it will be important for your patients to learn some important general hypnotic principles and techniques to be able to successfully utilize hypnotic philosophy: breathing patterns, the importance of language, and ability to recognize what is working about a specific hypnotic intervention and do more of it will be important for the clients. In this chapter I will review some important milestones in the birthing process, pointing out how they create a satisfying birthing experience for all parties involved.

IT'S HAPPENING

While preparation for the childbirth probably started several months before the anticipated delivery date, the practice of special techniques may intensify as the due date comes closer and closer on the mother's calendar. New sensations, such as pre-labor contractions, may bring additional anxiety, increasing the woman's practice of techniques she has rehearsed in the past months. This is a good time to reassure the future mother that these events and changes are natural, all part of the physiological capacities of her body and to validate her feelings by acknowledging that while expected, these events might be unsettling. Most of all, you can remind her that she has already learned and practiced hypnosis. She already knows how to do it. The important message to transmit is your confidence in her present abilities to implement what she has been practicing so far.

Why is it so important to get this message across, and why are you one of the best people to do it? To answer the first question, think back to your graduate studies and remember your endless nights preparing for the next important test. How did you know that you were ready for the test? What boosted your confidence? What allowed you to say, "Yes, I am ready"? For some people this moment never happens and they go to bed the night before the exam anxiety ridden. Others sense when studying more will be counterproductive and overtiring. Enough has been done. That translates to a feeling of confidence. Not an exaggerated confidence, but "I have just enough anxiety to stimulate me to pass the test well" confidence.

Addressing the experiential aspect of this learning, O'Hanlon and Martin (1992) write about the "class of problems vs. the class of solutions" model. Based on Ericksonian teaching, a hypnotherapist is invited to explore the client's problem and to come up with a specific intervention (an analogy, an anecdote, a task, a trance phenomenon). Once a positive experience is achieved with that, the hypnotist transfers the resolution to the context of the problem. In a sense, "you evoke it and then you *transfer* it across" (137).

In a similar way, once the expectant mother masters the skill of relaxation in an environment that is comforting, she can transfer that skill to a stressful and unfamiliar environment. Using the method described by O'Hanlon and Martin (1992), you can help the future mother to "*evoke* the relaxation" rather than "teach her relaxation" (137). She already knows what relaxation feels like; she just needs a cue to remind her of that feeling in the specific context.

The main advantage of this approach is that you help the future mother develop her own personalized experience of relaxation, rather than teaching her what feeling relaxed means to you. While we can share our experiences with others, we have to be mindful about our limited capacity to experience *exactly* what another person is experiencing. I am not speaking of empathy or our ability to relate to the experiences of another. Hopefully, no one in a helping profession is lacking that capacity. I am addressing our ability to physically and mentally relive what another person is living. Because of the biological and sociocultural uniqueness of each individual, we can only approximately perceive what another person is experiencing. Therefore, therapeutic interventions become more effective when the woman is helped to discover her own understanding, experience, and feelings of an event.

Just as you will remind the mother more than once that what she is experiencing is natural, I want to remind you more than once that you are the natural person to help your patients engage in self-discovery. You are "an expert," partly by your credentials and your perceived specialized knowledge of your field (for example, obstetrics). But if, in addition to being an excellent healthcare practitioner, you are able to be attentive to the fears, joys, and other experiences of your patients, you earn respect as an empathetic doctor who knows how to listen and direct your patients' exploration, validating and redirecting their experiences. Your words can have the power to induce specific hypnotic suggestions and help your patients engage in their own self-hypnosis.

As specific signs indicate that the delivery day is approaching, it is important to assure your patient that

- you and/or your staff are there to answer any of her questions;
- she already knows what she is doing; this is a good time to revisit her plan about what she will do when her water breaks, who will assist her when the labor begins, who is on her support team, and so on;
- she can continue practicing her techniques.

As the actual birth approaches, another technique you can use is one called "encouraging and restraining" (O'Hanlon and Martin 1992). In this, you encourage the woman to experience the future birthing event in a way that is appropriate to her. For example, while you encourage the pregnant woman to practice the techniques, you might tell her that she should only practice them when it feels comfortable and even tell her not to overdo it. Remember, you do not want the woman to expect that a specific practice will produce a specific effect. She will be setting herself up for disappointment. So you might advise her to go slowly and not to over practice, almost as an athlete or a ballet dancer is encouraged to rehearse but not overdo it before the final demonstration of their talent (note that I did not use the word "competition" or "performance"). The future mother is not competing with herself or with another pregnant woman. She is exploring different possibilities rather than rehearsing for a perfect birth. It is important to point out this difference to avoid her disappointment if the birth does not progress "as expected." (It never does.)

You may find the restraining part of the "encouraging and restraining" technique easier said than done. I understand. Several days before the birth of my daughter, I started to get impatient. Anxious about the due date, I kept thinking, "What if I do not know how to recognize that it is happening?" "What if I am far away from the place where I planned to give birth?" "What if my labor has to be induced?" Then on the day before my set due date, my water broke. It was 6 a.m. I went to the restroom and sat there quietly by myself collecting my thoughts. Something new was happening to my body. Then I went to the bedroom and woke up my husband. I told him that my water had broken. The next chapter in my life had just begun.

WHAT DO I DO NOW?

When I used to work in hospice, one of my colleagues, who was also my manager, would tell me, "We only die once, so we just have one attempt to make the experience right for the family." While we could not control what was happening to the dying person, we were able to explore what constituted the meaning of "a good death" for the family and, if possible, for the dying person and act accordingly.

The same can be said about the experience of giving birth. Your patient, this particular woman, will only birth this particular child once. She might have other children, but she will only birth once this child. The process of giving birth and its alignment with her expectations about how it was supposed to happen will influence and affect in various ways her self-image, her relationship with her newborn, her parenting style, and possibly her approach to her next birthing process if she chooses to have another child. Therefore, healthcare providers have great responsibility to assist the woman during her birthing process and to make it the best possible birth experience for her.

Although many women spend hours planning for this special moment, it is an understatement to say that the birth itself will be an utterly unique experience, because the sensations accompanying the process can't be adequately described in advance. Each woman has to experience them for the first time. Some methods, like those described in *HypnoBirthing*, encourage mothers not to listen to many stories of births, especially of births that did not go well, so that the women can construct their own image of the event.

All of us formulate our thoughts and speech unaware that we are using learned categories. Words, descriptions, dialogues are never neutral. They hold meaning and lead us to imagine our world in a certain way. They can form our experiences before we actually live them.

It is important for the caregiver to remind the mother that the coping skills that she developed during pregnancy while getting ready for the birth are not context dependent. In other words, she does not need to be in a particular environment, hold a particular posture, accompanied by a particular person, or listen to particular music to have a satisfying experience of her birth. All these elements can be helpful, but are not required, because she, the future mother, will create the context necessary for her own positive experience. Of course, it would be nice to be in the place that she selected to give birth (home, hospital, or birthing center), with her partner, doula, parents, or other trusted person. It is helpful to have the music that she chose for the occasion and to be able to move about as she planned (lie, sit, dance, and so on). Yes, it is all very helpful, but not required. These are just pieces of the bigger picture, in which each piece can be mentally recreated to best fit the actual event.

It is important for the mother to be prepared for the unexpected. When my water broke, I first called my doctor, and he told me to go to the hospital immediately. I knew that this would be his response, because in a medical context, when an OBGYN hears that the water has broken, they have to tell you to go to the hospital. Since I knew that I would not be allowed to eat before I gave birth, I ate a big breakfast at home. I wanted to concentrate on my sensations and experiences instead of being hungry, and I had no intention of trying to change the hospital culture. I then called my doula to inform her that I was going to the hospital and asked her to meet me there. She informed me that her other client was also in labor, and she would send me another doula. If I had been particularly attached to this person's presence and had seen it as a required condition for my successful birthing process, I would have been upset. However, I had not told myself that her presence was indispensable; therefore, I was not completely lost when she was unable to be there. Of course, this is one of the mildest unexpected things that could happen during birth. However, even little unexpected changes can trigger anxiety or discomfort in a woman who is about to give birth.

Therefore, remind the future mother that she can create the birthing environment almost anywhere she will be giving birth. Little things can help as much as big things to provide just enough context. For example, when I was preparing my suitcase for the hospital, which I did in advance, I included a few items that would remind me about my home, such as pillowcases. Again, they were not indispensable to recreate my home environment, which I could do by mentally evoking an image, a sense, or another attribute of my home. However, having reminders of home physically present was helpful.

When I arrived at the hospital for the childbirth, I also tried to get a sense of the hospital and what was expected from me. Mongan (2005) recommends putting a sign stating that the mother is having a hypnobirth, but I am hesitant to suggest that. Every hospital has its own culture and regulations set up to prevent medical errors and enhance efficiency. Nurses will respect the mother's wishes as long as they do not contradict rules and regulations of the hospital. However, a sign indicating hypnobirthing may set expectations on the patient's part and create more room for disagreement.

Knowing the hospital culture even a little can help the mother find a common language with the people working there. It is important to help her to establish such understanding, because it may make her experience more enjoyable. Physicians-obstetricians have a crucial role in providing this information to expectant mothers. Being insiders of the hospital culture, they can share just enough that the expectant mother won't be entering a completely unknown environment. This will save the women a lot of energy that can be better spent concentrating on their own sensations and experiences.

Being a healthcare provider myself, I feel privileged to know the hospital culture. For those who don't, the following information might be helpful:

- The hospital environment operates to create safety for everyone; thus it might seem somewhat impersonal. Not so long ago, hospitals were filthy places that generated as many diseases as they healed. Eventually precautions were taken to insure that everyone received standardized treatment. The uniformity that might seem cold and unwelcoming, is, in fact, a necessity for a spotless environment that provides the most efficient treatment possible (Shi and Singh 2008).
- Nurses are not uncaring; they are just very busy. It might seem to an untrained eye that nurses never spend enough time with the person. In fact, the nurses just cannot afford that luxury. They have many responsibilities to the hospital as well as to the patients, including keeping up-to-date records. Patients need to be aware of that fact and seek assistance of a doula if required.
- The physician will not be present for the largest part of the birthing process, usually arriving toward the end to deliver the baby. The woman can direct all her questions to the nursing staff, who are qualified to answer them or can call the doctor.

One of the myths about hypnosis is the necessity of a calm, relaxed environment to induce a trance (Yapko 1995). No special equipment (such as a pendulum), conditions, or quiet are necessary. I once helped someone with hypnosis in an ER, where beeping, crying, and yelling almost never stops. All the stimuli can be incorporated into the hypnotic suggestion. For example, when someone is focused on the noises in the background, the hypnotic suggestion might be, "and as you continue hearing all these different noises in the background, you will also start thinking about a special sensation developing in your right hand." Almost anything in the environment can be used as part of a suggestion. Thinking of hypnosis as improvisation rather than a set script is helpful to open possibilities for trance induction in any environment. Knowing the culture of the setting and being able to adjust to it can be tools for setting the stage for improvisation, including the birthing act itself.

TECHNIQUES IN ACTION

In chapter 6, I reviewed different strategies that might be helpful during the childbirth. Visualization, controlled breathing, and music are useful in creating the unique atmosphere that helps the birthing mother concentrate on her sensations and develop her own, most beneficial way to manage them for herself and her future baby. Equipped with all that information, the question remains, what is the best way to use various hypnotic techniques during the childbirth?

The first thing to remember is that although the techniques are presented sequentially, in the actual situation, there is no one way the different strategies have to be combined. Apart from the breathing techniques, which can be adapted to the different stages of labor, as recommended by Mongan (2005), the future mother, who has been practicing hypnotic techniques, can combine the modalities (and include additional ones) as she sees fit.

For example, an expectant mother can be encouraged to combine music and breathing techniques. She can actually use both strategies throughout the different stages of labor. As she will be practicing breathing techniques the whole time she is pregnant, she might find great comfort during delivery in controlling her breath in particular ways she has practiced. If she has practiced breathing techniques regularly and if they have brought her relief, different patterns of breathing will be almost second nature during the different phases of the childbirth. It is safe to say that breathing becomes such a focus of the woman's attention that it will take her attention away from her physical discomfort of the progression of contractions. This is what O'Hanlon and Martin (1992) describe as a distraction that is considered a helpful technique among other pain management strategies.

The second thing to remember is that while some signs and symptoms can indicate the progression of the labor, no one can tell the mother exactly how long it will take to give birth to her child. Thus, it will be helpful to advise your patient to find her own way to relax and move through the different stages, remaining confident in her body's ability to know the process. In fact, forgetting about different stages and concentrating on the birthing process itself might be her best strategy. Some future mothers become so preoccupied waiting for the opening of the cervix, for example, that they focus only on the lack of desired progress in that area. That can undermine the successful progression so desired by the woman in labor.

As discussed in the section about yoga (chapter 6), freedom from expectations allows yoga students to focus on their sensations in each moment. Expectations take us into a future that we cannot control. Hypnosis (similar to mindfulness in this case) holds us in the present moment, enabling us to explore its richness. It is often experiencing the present moment that facilitates a good outcome in the future.

For example, during my labor, when I was thinking about my cervix, I did not try to predict how much it would open in the next moment. Rather, I regularly used a technique of visualizing a flower blossoming or another nature metaphor. I became absorbed in doing this exercise, rather than in calculating how much benefit I'd get from it. I did it like a ritual, methodically and consciously following each step, staying in the moment with my image, which was changing as I was envisioning it.

Following the timeline of labor, it is important to remember that over time, the future mother becomes increasingly fatigued. Thus, it is wise to use certain strategies at the beginning of the labor process rather than toward the end. For instance, at the beginning of the labor, women are usually able to walk, dance, and move around the room to music they have selected, which may not be possible toward the end, during the second stage of labor.

Finally, remind the future mother to use the help of the person accompanying her—partner and/or doula—as she sees fit. During labor, partners want to ease the woman's discomfort, so it would be helpful to give them specific tasks as participants in the process. For example, if a partner is present in the room, he or she might choose to read visualization scripts that the expectant mother put together in preparation to the birth day. A partner might also be helpful in directing the doula and nurses and answering some of their questions that could take the mother's attention away from her experience. This would allow the mother in labor to concentrate on her own sensations without being interrupted. Finally, the partner might convey to nurses and other healthcare practitioners the woman's vision of the birth, encouraging everyone to use her preferred words whenever possible. The following word list has been adapted from Mongan's *HypnoBirth*, but you might work with the expectant mother to add any words that fit with her image about labor and delivery:

> Contractions: Wave
> Delivery: Birthing
> Due Date: Birthing Time
> Pain or Contractions: Pressure/Tightening
> Pushing: Birth Breathing
> Complications: Special Circumstances
> Bloody Show: Birth Show
> Dilating: Opening
> Fetus: Unborn Baby
> Braxton-Hicks: Pre-labor warm-ups

One important word to attend to is "pain." Widely used in the medical environment, during childbirth the word often connotes unbearable discomfort that is supposed to be managed with specific medical interventions (for example, epidural). While I do not deny the possible presence of pain during the labor, I do believe that the perception of pain (and other sensations) depends on the words we use to describe our feelings. Should your patient prefer to use different descriptions to structure her birthing environment, it will be important to emphasize that she and her birthing team can develop a firm belief that this is how she is choosing to see her childbirth. It will be also important to understand that not everyone on the medical team will be accepting of this approach. Thus, without the woman's own team, repetition is important.

However, what if the future mother herself uses the word "pain" to describe her experiences? How can you help her alleviate painful sensations by using hypnosis? Depending on the kind of pain she describes, different techniques can be used to manage the different sensations. It is important to not take the word "pain" as an actual description. The meaning of pain varies greatly from one person to another, as well as the ability to manage painful sensations (on a scale from 1 to 10, 1 and 10 do not feel the same for different people).

In some way the technique of renaming provides the possibility of reinterpreting the whole pain-associated environment. However, some women may feel that changing the name of their sensations minimizes their feelings and experiences. In this case, reinterpretation may not work. For instance, using the word "tightening" instead of "contraction" to alter the woman's perceptions and physiological process may not work because the word change does not sufficiently describe the sensation for some women.

In these cases, techniques such as the hypnotic technique of anesthesia (defined by O'Hanlon and Martin [1992] as "lack of feeling in all or part of the body" [177]), analgesia ("lack of pain in all or part of the body" [177]), pain displacement ("putting the pain in another location in the body or in the world" [177]), or time distortion ("expanding the subjective experience of time when the person feels more comfortable and condensing time when the person feels pain" [177]) might be more appropriate. Again, it is important to first explore the sensations with the future mother, their locations, and their depth, to work with her to either dim the pain or to relocate the pain.

In *HypnoBirthing,* Mongan (2005) describes specific techniques that allude to the above-mentioned methods. The first method is called Glove Relaxation: "Imagine that you are putting a soft, silver glove onto your right hand—a special glove of natural endorphins. Immediately, the fingers of your hand begin to feel larger and to tingle, as though there were springs at the ends of your fingers. The silver glove, with its endorphins flowing around your fingers, your palm and the back of your hand will cause your hand to feel numb, the way it would if you were to place it into a large container of icy slush" (152). Once the feeling is acquired in the hand, the patient then can transfer this feeling to different parts of her body, being able to spread the feeling of numbness and comfort.

Another technique, called Time Distortion, invites the woman to give herself a suggestion that five minutes now seems as only one minute. An expectant mother would first have to bring herself in a state of relaxation and then try this technique. This exercise can also involve the birthing partner, who can provide similar suggestions to the mother in labor.

There are a variety of techniques to help the birthing mother address her sensations by softening them. Such exercise might involve a color, so that the future mother experiments with the intensity of the color, the lighter color paralleling a lighter sensation. The pain might be also envisioned on a "Depthometer," by which a painful sensation can become lighter and lighter as the woman counts down or up, whichever feels more in line with her sensation.

Throughout the process of giving birth, it can be also helpful for the doula to notice the techniques that the patient is using and validate their effectiveness. When I started my second stage of labor, my first hypno-birth doula was able to join me. Since I had not been able to practice the final method of breathing, hearing my doula tell me I was doing it correctly was reassuring and encouraged me to engage that breathing method even more. Such reassuring presence and validation, which can be provided by anyone on the medical team, can be beneficial by allowing the woman in labor to concentrate on her own sensations and to receive validation and encouragement from her healthcare providers.

Just before I gave birth, I had an unpleasant situation that could have been avoided had I trusted my body and had the physician been more mindful of the effect of his actions on my perception and subsequent physiological response. The baby was coming out, and the physician was standing in a position to receive the baby. He was very helpful in the process, allowing me to try different positions and even using a rope to promote more movement on my part. Suddenly, he looked at his watch; I looked around and saw several surgical instruments on the table. One of my main fears, which he knew, was having an episiotomy. I reacted with fear and I had a tear. It wasn't bad, but I believe that it could have been avoided.

This situation illustrates again the powerful connection between the body, mind, and spirit. I got scared, because I interpreted certain actions of the physician in a certain way. It is possible that he was not even thinking of proceeding with an episiotomy, but as I was so highly aware of my environment and had my own fears, I interpreted his behavior in line with my own preconceptions. This situation also illustrates how important it is to talk to your patient, encouraging her and explaining your steps. This will help her to have the experience that she has been working to achieve.

EIGHT

Hypnotic Assistance in the Unexpected

When I first learned about hypnosis in graduate school, its powerful premises took me aback. It seems that the connection promoted between the body and the mind cannot be ignored once we start looking at the world through the hypnotic lens. To paraphrase de Shazer (1994), words became truly magic: I could sense how the utilization of a specific word or a preference for a specific question could determine a new avenue for a therapeutic conversation. The influence of hypnosis seemed very powerful, almost too powerful. That sense made hypnosis feel overwhelming at times, especially when I started practicing it and realized that more than half of my clients considered hypnosis as a magic pill that would cure their long-term struggles in one session. It was hard to make them realize that while hypnosis can have a powerful influence on a person's life, there are other factors that we have to take into consideration when implementing hypnosis. In the case of hypnobirth, some physical manifestations that might accompany pregnancy (for example, early pregnancy toxicosis, medical complications, or pre-existing conditions) are variables that would modify the initial intentions and introduce a different outcome of the well-thought-out pregnancy and birthing scenarios.

What I often explained to my clients, and what I think also applies in the case of hypnobirth, is the fact that even if everything does not go as planned, hypnotic techniques can be beneficial and provide important assistance to expectant mothers, their partners, and healthcare providers. In this chapter, I examine specific unplanned situations during pregnancy, delivery, and postpartum that benefit from hypnosis, even if the utilized techniques or interventions are used to respond to a different need.

HYPNOSIS AND SYMPTOM MANAGEMENT

While some pregnancies go smoothly, others remain particularly memorable for the specific symptoms that become associated with this particular period of the woman's life. I can imagine certain providers reading the preceding chapters and thinking, "All of this is great, but what do I say to a woman who complains about morning nausea or who has pains in her lower back that will not subside? What specific interventions can I recommend even before I encourage her to try meditation or to relax enough to explore self-hypnosis?"

Though I often hesitate to compare pregnancy to any other medical condition (since the future mother is not sick) and the changes in the body are usually expected and manageable, I can definitely support the fact that specific characteristics of hypnosis have been developed for symptom management and can be applied effectively during pregnancy and delivery. For example, Bioy and Wood (2006) underline that "one of the peculiarities of hypnosis is that it is concerned with both the somatic and the neurological, with the physiology and psychology, all at the same time and in the same place—the consultation room" (119). This focus of hypnosis is well suited with the philosophy of soothing gentle care so much needed during these moments of women's lives. In a way, "hypnosis allows patients to change not so much their objective situation as the way in which they experience pain or life on a subjective level. They create a new reality for themselves; they reinvent their present by learning to alter their body perceptions" (118).

One of the most documented applications of hypnosis is in pain management (Bioy and Wood 2006; Caracappa 1963; Douglas 1999; Iglesias 2004; Pan, Morrison, Ness, and Fugh-Berman 2000; Willard 1974). The conceptualization of pain includes physical pain, emotional pain, spiritual pain, anxiety, fear, and depression (Marino 2009). It is often helpful to consider McCaffrey's (1999) definition of pain as "whatever the experiencing person says it is, existing whenever he says it does" (as cited by Marino). This definition of pain, which refuses to apply "traditional dualism separating mind from body or mind from matter" (Bioy and Wood 1972, xi) represents a relational understanding of the human experience.

One of the first descriptions of hypnotherapy for the relief of pain in a patient with life-threatening illness was offered by Milton Erickson (1959). He provided illustrations of three successful cases of hypnosis conducted with patients suffering from pain. Rooted in the technique of utilization, described later by Zeig (1994) as the "readiness of the therapist to respond strategically to any and all aspects of the patient or the environment" (298), the hypnotherapist constructed his hypnotic intervention based on the symptomatology presented by the patient. Erickson defined this approach as a way to use "a patient's own mental processes in a way that are outside of his usual range of intentional or voluntary control" (Erickson, Rossi, and Rossi, as cited in de Shazer 1988, 113). For example, in one of the cases, the patient's feeling of weakness was utilized to reorient his attention from the somatic sensations. Moreover, Erickson emphasized that pain can be changed through anesthesia, analgesia, and/or amnesia. By modifying the person's relationship to the problem by changing the person's sensations or memories about the painful sensations, Erickson changed the patient's experiences.

Since pain might be present before and during labor, it is important to explore with the expectant mother her understanding and experience of pain sensations. Some questions to explore might include the location of pain, the intensity of the pain, the description of the pain (consider asking for a metaphor that could be utilized to describe the mother's sensations), and the cessation of pain (are there any times when the pain is not present?). The presence of pain can be daunting for a mother during her pregnancy. If the pain occurs before labor and the assessment shows that the future mother is safe to utilize hypnosis for pain management, encourage your patient to get in touch with a hypnotherapist to develop effective techniques for pain management. If the pain occurs during labor, it may be very disappointing to the future mother who was planning to experience a natural birth with assistance of hypnosis but instead needs some medical assistance, such as an epidural. Addressing the sensation of pain experienced during labor, Gabriel (2011) explains that there are in general three levels of pain intensities that might be experienced by women: "Some women feel no pain. Others feel pain, but it is never stronger than a strong menstrual cramp. Others feel pain so intense that it requires much focused effort to get through. Still others feel pain so excruciating that they are traumatized, even to the point of having fearful flashbacks years later" (102). According to Gabriel, most women fall into the third category and are able to develop techniques to manage their pain symptoms. In any event, it is important to take a few moments to process the mother's experience of birthing should it go unplanned; reassurance and normalization are as important as the simple validation of the mother's feelings. Often a provider can make a big difference just by listening carefully to what the mother has to say about her pain, without offering any specific advice.

Considering the case of excruciating pain, Gabriel notes that this type of pain is often prompted by some accompanying mental health condition, such as anxiety or depression (Gabriel 2011). Such conceptualization points to the connection between physical and emotional pain, which often feed each other—especially if a pregnant woman is in her second or third pregnancy and a previous pregnancy was associated with traumatic or unpleasant experiences. For example, a woman might have apprehension about a possible C-section if she experienced a C-section in the past, and such apprehension might lead to the development of anxious or fearful behavior that might influence her pregnancy. Should you encounter such a situation, it is important to refer the patient to a hypnotherapist to address the experienced symptoms. Hypnosis can also be utilized in combination with other complementary and alternative medicine (CAM) modalities, such as acupuncture, massage therapy, aromatherapy, psychotherapy, behavior therapy, imagery, cognitive coping strategies, music therapy, botanicals, meditation, yoga, and distant healing.

It is also important to emphasize that in using an Ericksonian approach, a hypnotherapist builds on the client's strengths and possibilities, rather than trying to understand the cause of an existing problem. In this approach, a hypnotherapist might not necessarily utilize a former trance induction, but instead reframe the situation, presenting a symptom in a different light. For example, in a famous case known as the case of an African-violet lady (Haley 1993), Milton Erickson encountered an older person who was referred to him because she was depressed. Erickson went to visit the woman and was invited to see the house. Since the client was quite rich, the house was well put together, but it looked abandoned. As he viewed the house, he noticed a beautiful flower and became curious about its origins. The woman stated that she used to grow African violets but felt so depressed lately that she did not have the energy for that any longer. Erickson looked at the woman and informed her that she was not so much depressed as selfish. He instructed her to start growing the flowers again immediately and to start looking for occasions where people were in need of the flowers (e.g., christenings, baptisms, funerals, etc.). The lady did what Erickson prescribed. She started looking for events and supplying them with flowers. As a result, her social connections grew, and she became less and less depressed. When she passed away, many people in Milwaukee gathered for her funeral. This case is a typical illustration of the Ericksonian approach to treatment. Erickson was curious enough to determine what was important for the patient and then utilized it for her advantage. The patient did not experience a trance but felt connected enough to the hypnotherapist to implement his suggestions, which ultimately made a difference.

It is important to remember that often what we say to our patients and clients matters as much as how we say it. In the case of an expectant mother, the validation of her worries and acknowledging that her worries represent her care for the baby and her willingness to give the best to her baby might be just enough to make a difference in the mother's feelings and behaviors. It is vital to concentrate on the mother's strengths and her ability to do things right. Noticing at least one positive way she is able to manage her stress and be mindful about her unborn baby can go a long way to establish a therapeutic alliance and powerful connection between the expectant mother and her healthcare provider. After all, Erickson just noticed one flower, resulting in the woman growing the whole garden.

Considering hypnosis for symptom management, it is important to realize that hypnosis "orients you and your clients *alongside*, rather than vis-à-vis, their symptoms, allowing you to discover together, in the moment, how this particular sensory-based chunk of experience, right *here*, and/or that one right *there* . . . can begin little by little to shift" (Flemons 2008, 16). To understand the effectiveness of hypnosis, we have to keep in mind Bateson's (2000) thesis that we make sense of our world by making connections and drawing differences among the various components. For example, to differentiate different smells, we need to notice the different fragrances and give them different names. In addition, we usually associate the fragrances with specific circumstances or contexts. For example, the smell of burning paper is usually associated with danger and is considered unpleasant, while the smell of bread cooking in the oven is associated with home comfort and pleasant feelings.

As we accumulate experiences, we build more and more associations, some of which become quite automatic. We don't have to think twice before describing certain sensations or feelings. After all, these connections are necessary to our functioning. However, such links become burdensome when they are associated with a particular symptom. Instead of remaining curious about the manifestation of a symptom, we try to eliminate it, which often leads to the establishment of greater association. By trying to get rid of a symptom, we start noticing it even more. For example, try right now to not think about a pink panther, and you will notice that you can only think about a pink panther.

To establish new connections, the hypnotherapist invites the client to do just the opposite of not thinking about the symptom and instead become curious about the symptom. In this context, curiosity does not mean acceptance. The patient does not have to accept the symptom; rather the client is invited to explore the characteristics of the symptom. The more she engages in that exploration, the more her perception of the symptom will start to change. The change happens because of the multiple relationships the client is establishing while she contemplates the symptom. For example, if the woman is experiencing nausea, she might be asked to explore all the different feelings that she has while feeling nauseated, her ability to control or provoke such feelings, or her ability to relate these feelings to different contexts. It is through the exploration that the change happens.

Hypnotic techniques might also be instrumental in addressing any complications during pregnancy, such as high blood pressure or premature labor. These conditions often require bed rest and sometimes significantly impact the quality of life of an expectant mother, who finds herself restrained, anxious, and bored for several months preceding delivery. Hypnosis can be helpful in these situations by assisting the future mother to relax despite the medical condition that she is experiencing. The relaxation diminishes her stress, which positively affects her overall well-being and that of her unborn baby. Different techniques of visualization described by Mongan (2005) allow expectant mothers to get in touch with their bodies and with their babies. For example, the opening bud visualization technique can be used in reverse to prevent the ripening of the cervix. Future mothers also can be instructed to talk to their babies about their love, their care, and the necessity to wait a little bit longer before arriving. By engaging in such conversation (in a gentle tone of voice, concentrating on her connection with the baby), the future mother is engaging in self-hypnosis, which helps her to get in touch with her own feelings and sensations.

On the other hand, hypnosis can be used not to slow labor but to induce labor, when nature needs a little help (Mongan 2005). Relaxation can be useful the other way around. By calming her mind, releasing the tension from her body, the patient allows herself to go into labor. Some specific visualization techniques, like a blossom blooming and opening, can induce labor as well. It is especially helpful to combine visualization techniques with breathing techniques.

Of course, it is very important to emphasize to your patient that any unusual symptoms, such as bleeding, an excessive amount of meconium, severe headaches, and the like, should be checked with a medical provider before trying any hypnosis-based techniques.

C-SECTION: DOES HYPNOSIS STILL HAVE A PLACE?

Often when I discuss the capacity of a hypnotic mindset and usefulness of hypnotic techniques, I hear women say, "It sounds interesting, but I had a C-section," as if a complication during delivery would rule out the use of hypnosis. In public consciousness, "hypnobirth" often means "natural birth." As we saw in chapter 2, the history of hypnobirthing and natural child birthing overlaps. However, these movements have separate histories, and the first applications of hypnosis pertained to pain management. Therefore, not only can hypnosis be utilized during complications, you can recommend it as a viable complementary intervention for future mothers who have been practicing hypnosis during their pregnancy, as well as a coping strategy for family and professional caregivers who assist future mothers during delivery.

A friend and colleague of mine was planning for a hypnobirth, only to find out at the last moment that she had to have an emergency C-section. Her disappointment was great, but after reflecting back on her experience, she said that her practice of hypnosis all during the pregnancy helped her remain calm and centered on the birth of her child, rather than be completely overwhelmed by the circumstances. "Even if you could not tell from the outside," she says, "I was able to concentrate on my attention and did not completely panic. I was not able to have a hypnobirth, but I was able to benefit from hypnotic techniques to deal with a stressful, unexpected surgery."

This account is important in light of the fact that most women who experience an unplanned C-section feel lonely, frightened, or traumatized (Gabriel 2011). "Each complication requires quick acceptance of a change in plans and expectations, often without a complete understanding of the situation" (Simkin 2008, 267).

If a woman had planned to have a vaginal birth, she might experience a sense of failure if she has a C-section. While in surgery, women can be overwhelmed by the sterile nature of the OR and a procedure that involves partial anesthesia. Some women are frightened that they might accidentally feel "too much" during the surgery.

Several hypnotic techniques can be initiated while in the OR to help the future mother to relax, including visualization, controlled breathing, and meditation. It is important to find out what has worked well during the pregnancy and reinforce the utilization of those techniques. Several mothers I spoke to mentioned that they felt objectified while in surgery. These feelings were often intensified by the non-responsiveness of the medical personnel, who treated the future mother as if she were unconscious, instead of reassuring her and normalizing the situation. This attitude of medical providers contributed to the feeling of irrelevance and in some cases to the development of posttraumatic stress reactions (Gabriel 2011; Ryding, Wijma, and Wijma 1997).

To help future mothers to thrive through this experience, medical providers have to be extremely careful to utilize the resources of the patient, including her ability to meditate. It would be helpful if, while creating a Birthing Plan, women noted that it is acceptable to deviate from the plan if necessary for a better outcome for the mother and the baby. And it is also important to remember throughout the surgery what feelings the woman might experience. Does she feel afraid for her or her baby due to the anesthesia? Does she feel displaced and frightened by the OR environment? Would she like more information about the whole process of assisted delivery? Finally, remember that after the surgery is over, mothers can experience signs of posttraumatic stress several months after the delivery. You can encourage mothers in this situation to engage in hypnotic practice or to seek the help of a trained hypnotherapist.

PARTNERS DURING LABOR: HYPNOSIS STILL WORKS

Books have been written about the important role of a partner during pregnancy and delivery (England and Horowitz 1998; Mongan 2005). When addressing particularly challenging moments of women facing pregnancy and birth complications, Simkin (2008) states that a supportive team can make a difference and that partners are of primary importance in providing assistance to expectant mothers. While an abundance of literature provides guidance on how partners can be involved in helping the future mother face different moments during pregnancy and delivery, the research pertaining to the support of family and professional caregivers is still in its infancy.

Reflecting on emotions shared by fathers, England and Horowitz (1998) noted that the experience of men who assisted the future mother in labor could be profound and life changing. The authors encourage mental health providers to explore the meaning of pregnancy and birth with future fathers. These explorations are necessary for all partners who accompany a woman in delivery, including non-biological moms in a lesbian couple or a close family friend (male or female) who accompanies a single mother during labor. This is especially important because the needs of these couples are often unrecognized or minimized (McManus, Hunter, and Renn 2006).

This thinking about the meaning of pregnancy and birth by the partner becomes even more crucial if one considers the impact of complications on the partner's perception of labor and the influence of a stressful situation even after the situation is resolved. Some mothers who experienced a C-section shared with me that in that stressful time during the delivery, they had been completely absorbed in their attention on the needs of the baby, sometimes without realizing the gravity of the situation. Later they found out that their partners had experienced the shock of facing the fear of losing their loved one. The partners were left to experience their emotions on their own. Without any guidance, they remained in a sense of stupor or hyperarousal long after the dangerous situation was resolved. Their memories about the birth were unpleasant if not traumatic.

Considering that the partner is often a vital part of completing a hypnobirth (for example, it is often the partner who assists in reading a script with hypnotic suggestions), it is safe to assume that partners are already familiar with the foundations of hypnosis. Therefore, it is important to remind the partners of their knowledge of this coping mechanism in the midst of the chaos that often accompanies an unplanned medical intervention. By practicing visualization (of a successful outcome, for example) and breathing techniques of relaxation, partners can leave the OR feeling calmer even though the birth did not go as expected.

PROFESSIONAL CAREGIVERS: HYPNOSIS FOR WOUNDED HEALERS?

The utilization of hypnosis as part of the coping strategies for the medical staff (such as physicians, nurses, doulas, and so on) is poorly documented. What is known is the long-lasting effect of traumatic birth experiences on medical personnel and the paucity of training to help medical providers process such experiences (Pastor Montero, Romero Sanchez, and Hueso Montoro 2011). Nonetheless, several studies pointed out the importance of attending to physicians' experiences of burnout and compassion fatigue to enhance the quality of care for patients and to create a satisfying working experience among healthcare providers (Embracio, Papazian, Kentish-Barnes, Pochard, and Azoulay 2007; Kearney, Weininger, and Vachon 2009).

To address the need for self-care among medical practitioners, Jon Kabat-Zinn pioneered the concept of mindfulness in the 1970s, by creating a Center of Mindfulness in Medicine, Health Care, and Society at the University of Massachusetts Medical School. The center is dedicated to providing mindfulness training to medical professionals and conducting research on the influence of this training. Research has demonstrated that the practice of mindfulness is not only an effective tool to minimize negative experiences, but also a potential way toward personal and professional growth and resilience (Novak 1999). However, even though mindfulness can be part of a hypnotic experience, hypnosis is not synonymous with mindfulness and possesses its own benefits, such as more intentional movements toward change rather than observation of specific events and their influence.

To address the needs of professional caregivers and examine the usefulness of hypnosis, Curtis (2001) investigated the use of hypnotherapy with healthcare providers. To remediate the paucity of research in this area and investigate the use of hypnosis in the relief of symptoms among healthcare providers, the researcher offered one session of hypnosis a week, for an hour, to each participant. The duration of the study was five months and included eleven employees. Curtis utilized three questionnaires to collect the data: one weekly evaluation that reviewed clients' experience of each session, one assessment at the end of the study that provided an overall perception of the benefit, and a client-satisfaction survey. At the end of the study, 91 percent of clients reported perceived benefits, such as feelings of relaxation and calmness, being de-stressed and empowered, and having increased confidence and energy. Many of the participants expressed a desire to know more about hypnosis.

While more research is needed to develop practical guidelines for hypnosis utilization among healthcare providers, the following recommendations can help you initiate the practice or spark your curiosity about this self-care opportunity:

- Follow the example of your clients: breathing, visualization, and relaxation techniques practiced by expectant women have a general benefit and can be utilized by healthcare professionals as well.
- Start your day with a self-hypnotic practice, reflecting on what you would like to achieve and how you are planning to go about it.

- Finish your day with a five- to ten-minute relaxation reflecting on what you were able to achieve, giving yourself praise for what you were able to do and forgiving yourself for some things that you were not able to accomplish.

Small steps can lead to big changes. By practicing what you recommend to your patients, you not only engage in a better self-care, but you also learn more about hypnosis and its effects. This will help you realize the benefits and limitations of this technique and recommend it knowledgeably to your patients.

NINE

Life after Giving Birth

The birth of a baby transforms lives. After months of planning and antici-
pating, the baby and the parents will be going through a period of adjustment filled with joy and happiness, but also with worries and doubts.
Even the most rigorous preparations cannot anticipate the full picture of
the experiences and sensations accompanying the birth and the first
months after. New routines and rituals will be put in place to reflect the
birth of the new family. In the meantime, the day-to-day routine will
create a comfortable zone for the baby, providing her with security while
feeling in proximity to the people she loves.

While hypnosis was helpful in preparing the parents to welcome the
newborn, the continuous utilization of the familiar hypnotic techniques
and philosophy has proved to be helpful in this important period of
adjustment: the first steps toward motherhood and breastfeeding.

NEW FAMILY

The exciting day that the mother has anticipated for months has arrived
and passed. A new person has been born and the new family has formed
as a result of this baby's arrival. While long-awaited and expected, this
transformation from a couple to a family can be stressful for new parents.
In fact, much needs to be learned: how to interact with the newborn, how
to interact with each other, how to prioritize among individual needs and
family needs? All these questions will become part of the new routine,
but also will cause an ongoing effort to find the balance between individual needs, the couple's romance, and the family life. Is this another arena
in which hypnosis can be helpful? How can the philosophy and techniques developed prior to the birth help parents during this new phase in
their lives?

While the biological part of the process is well under way, the emotional, social, and spiritual formation will continue long after the baby is born. As the parents' medical provider and team member, you can advise the newly formed family to continue exploring the important benefits of hypnosis as they build the foundations of their family relationships. Although the first few months of the baby's life will pass by quickly, they will be exhausting for the parents. It is known that among all mammals, human babies are the most helpless when they are born, being completely dependent on their parents for their survival (Sears 2013). Baby deer can walk a few hours after birth, but human babies cannot even hold their heads up for the first few months after birth. Babies are born unprepared to face the outside world that is so different from the dark, humid, closeted environment they inhabited the previous nine months. The outside world is a completely new, anxiety-provoking, unpredictable environment. Need for human warmth and human interaction is as vital for the baby as their need for food. In fact, human presence continues to provide the newborn with the attributes of the maternal womb for at least three months after birth, providing the time to develop coping mechanisms to survive in this new atmosphere (Karp 2003). These few months may also determine future interactions between the baby and the mother, as expectations formed by each can influence their responses moving forward.

The mother's constant need to be physically and emotionally near her baby can become overwhelming, as can the anxiety caused by her sense of responsibility and attempts to meet the needs of the infant. It takes time to learn the personality of this new human being and to develop new skills of mothering. I remember when the nurse first handed my newborn daughter to me. She placed the little bundle in my hands and left the room. There I was, holding this creature who was not even able to hold her own head up, and suddenly I realized that I did not know how to change position from one hand to another. I thought that I could inadvertently hurt my baby by moving her. So I called the nurse for help. I was overwhelmed by the feeling of responsibility toward this little baby who was utterly dependent on me.

Being overwhelmed for a few minutes by feelings of amazement and gratitude is stimulating, unless it grows into panic or an anxiety-laden stupor. As the woman's provider, you can remind her that being present for someone else first requires being present for yourself. Just as she did during pregnancy and birthing, the new mother can use hypnosis to draw on her own resources to develop a balanced attitude toward her experiences of demands and her responses to fulfill those demands. After all, when we are completely submerged by our own feelings, we are unable to understand, let alone empathize with, another's feelings.

It is important for the mother to start exploring a number of questions in this new stage of her life:

- What does it mean for her to be a mother?
- What are her needs? What are the baby's needs? Where do the two overlap? Where do they separate?
- What is the mother doing for herself in order to take the best care of her baby?
- What are the mother's experiences of her interactions with the baby?
- What are her experiences of being a mother?

The mother may choose to explore these questions on her own, with her partner, or with a professional. Nonetheless, by engaging in the self-hypnosis techniques she has already learned, she can access peace and relaxation even in the middle of the most hectic and emotionally challenging day. The same techniques that she used as your patient to prepare herself to give birth she can now use when the baby is crying uncontrollably or when the mother is physically and emotionally exhausted. And if she practices the techniques well before becoming overwhelmed, she can avoid completely that sense of impending breakdown.

Consider reviewing with your patient chapter 5, on finding her element, practicing the breathing techniques, and finding time to use forms of guided imagery or visualization. Or remind her of the techniques she had become adept at before the baby was born. These self-hypnotic exercises can help the new mother appreciate her interactions with the newborn, because she now can be present for this little being. Meaningful interactions born from a calm, peaceful state will also be beneficial to the newborn, not only creating reassurance and security, but also providing a moment to build deep connections with one of the most important human beings in his/her life, the mother.

A few words have to be said about the needs of partners as well. The mother benefits from the supportive hormones associated with breastfeeding that provide additional energy. However, partners may feel even greater physical exhaustion. Not only that, they may have a sense of having been left aside. The attention has dramatically shifted from the partner to the baby, limiting the time the new parents can be together. The change to the new day-to-day routine is also unsettling for mother and father. These and a myriad of other changes that the new father or mother's partner experiences need to be faced and understood. Among the questions you can raise for him, as well as for the new mother, to consider over time include:

- How is he/she coping with his/her new role?
- How does he/she perceive his/her position in the new family structure?
- What memories and old emotions are brought up by this new situation?

- How can he/she continue to find and enjoy the little moments with his/her partner?
- How can each of them relax, breathe, connect, and develop?
- How will both parents continue to transform, creating a strong foundation for their new unit?

The birth of the child is just the first link in a long chain of connections the parents will develop with this new person, starting from their first love and continuing with the development of a profound understanding of each other's needs and responsibilities. The questions posed in this chapter are not meant to be answered once and finally. They require the conscious awareness of the mind-body connection that will have to be continuously developed long after the birth of the child. In that sense, the philosophical understanding and specific techniques of hypnosis acquired before the childbirth can be considered as the foundation for further exploration of the self with a hypnotherapist or by the self-hypnosis learned previously.

FIRST BREASTFEEDING

One of the reasons women explore the possibilities of hypnosis for birthing is to enhance the connection with their infant at the moment of birthing. Building that special bond with the child thus starts with the first wave of contraction. However, continuing to build that connection will become the work of motherhood. Each mother finds her special way to be with her baby. Starting to breastfeed their newborn offers just one more opportunity to add another layer of love to this construction of a special relationship. However, breastfeeding does not always come easily.

The physiological benefits of breastfeeding have been stressed by multiple authors (Mongan 2005; Sears 2000) and by the World Health Organization (2014), which places breastfeeding as the first option for the baby's nutrition and recommends two years of breastfeeding as optimal. It has been determined that breast milk has special substances that help build babies' immune systems, preventing the development of diseases and facilitating optimal growth (Cerini and Aldrovandi 2013; Rabet, Vos, Boehm, and Garssen 2008).

In addition to these biological attributes and the obvious financial advantage of breast milk being free compared to often-expensive baby formula, breastfeeding offers an additional opportunity to connect with the baby by satisfying his ultimate need for security in this unfamiliar and often scary world. Researchers have pointed out that colostrum, the first substance that appears just after the baby is born and just before the actual milk, has the same odor and taste as the amniotic fluid (Schaal, Marlier, and Soussignan 2000). This is nature's wise way of providing continuity between the environment of the mother's womb and the new world of the baby. Without words, the mother can immediately reassure her baby that while the environment has changed, some things haven't: She will continue to take care of the baby by satisfying the basic needs for food and security. To this date, researchers have not been able to reproduce in a formula either the special characteristic of the colostrum nor the unique substance of breast milk that allows the optimal development of the immune system.

In addition to the biological advantages of the breastfeeding, an emotional connection develops during breastfeeding: the mother is learning to recognize the cues the baby gives her and as a consequence is beginning to learn her baby's expressions (Sears 2000). For example, while the baby mostly lets everyone know about his or her discomfort by crying, the mother will eventually learn that different types of crying correspond to the baby's different needs (Karp 2003). By learning this baby language, the mother will respond faster to her baby's requests, reinforcing the baby's understanding that her mother will take care of her.

Breastfeeding not only benefits babies, it also benefits mothers. Biologically, mothers who breastfeed run a lower risk of uterine hemorrhaging following birth, a lower risk of developing ovarian and breast cancer, and have lower blood sugar levels (Dermer 1998; do Carmo França-Botelho, Carvalho Ferreira, França, França, and Honorio-França 2012). The psychological effects of breastfeeding on mothers are also well documented (Dermer 2001). The skin-to-skin interaction reinforces the special connection between a mother and her child; lactation supports the release of specific hormones that appear to produce calmness in the mother, and a well-developing baby tends to improve the mother's sense of self-worth and self-confidence in her new role.

Despite all the benefits of breastfeeding and its natural advantages for both parties involved, breastfeeding often does not come naturally to mothers. In fact, the first experiences of breastfeeding are often painful, or at least uncomfortable, to the new mother. The mother needs to learn how to feed her baby, how often to breastfeed, and how to practice different positions to discover the most comfortable one for her and her baby.

It is also important to underscore that the milk supply is often related to the mother's level of comfort and her emotional state. Fear, for example, tends to diminish milk production. I remember a time when my mother was breastfeeding my brother and was scared by a rooster's aggressiveness outside the cottage where we were spending the summer. The shock of the rooster's attack led to her complete loss of milk for two days. But it's not just fear that can affect the flow of milk. If the infant cannot suckle efficiently, the mother may respond with uneasiness about breastfeeding, which can diminish the milk supply. Therefore, it is important to follow up with your patients regarding their ability to breastfeed and offer them the assistance of a lactation specialist if needed.

Breastfeeding creates a special connection between the mother and the child, which the mother can reinforce by establishing her own special connection between her body (being ready to perform this unique act of love) and her mind (being ready to accept the new possibilities of the body). Because hypnosis deepens the woman's mind/body/emotions connections, it is natural that hypnotic philosophy and techniques can benefit the lactating mother breastfeeding her baby or experiencing difficulties breastfeeding (Molyneaux 2013).

You can help your patient who is new to breastfeeding or perhaps having difficulty by offering hypnotic suggestions and techniques, such as the following:

- Breastfeeding *is* a natural act. Despite the fact that her breastfeeding techniques will improve as she repeatedly feeds her child, the mother already has the natural ability to breastfeed.
- The milk flow will increase if the mother feels relaxed. Remember that just telling ourselves we are relaxed can make us feel more stressed. The baby's crying or the mother's exhaustion after a sleepless night does not contribute to relaxation. Some of the relaxation techniques that your patient learned in preparation for childbirth can be helpful in achieving relaxation. Visualization can work especially well. If your patient wants to try this technique, you can help her develop specific images that allude to a free flow, such as waterfalls or flowing creeks. When she has decided on the image that works for her, encourage her to bring the vivid image to mind a few minutes before each breastfeeding.
- Breastfeeding is often associated with the sense of being a good mother. You can suggest to the woman that she can use positive affirmations pertaining to her new role as a mother, reassuring herself that she is a "good-enough mother" and that her ability to connect with her baby is becoming stronger with each day. Another helpful exercise is to ask the mother to write three specific things that she has done for herself and her baby that contribute to a stronger connection. The mother can then develop a list of affirmations based on these prompts, or build the list by adding an item every week or every month.

Most importantly, mothers need to be reassured and reminded that breastfeeding is one of the most beautiful gifts that a mother can offer to her child. As my first pediatrician told me, "The baby just needs to start; you will then never be able to stop her." I breastfed my daughter for three years, though the last two years could be characterized more as nursing than feeding. By responding to the basic needs of their children, mothers allow them not only to connect with us, but also to be open to their connection with the world, one step at a time. Self-hypnosis promotes that connection.

MOTHERHOOD

The end of pregnancy welcomes the beginning of motherhood. This new period in your patients' lives will bring many transitions, discoveries, and new responsibilities. It will be overwhelming, exciting, and challenging all at the same time. A quote attributed to Elizabeth Stone, the author of *A Boy I Once Knew* (2002), states, "making a decision to have a child—it is momentous. It is to decide forever to have your heart go walking around outside your body" (25). This invisible connection that started developing when the baby was still in the womb, with care, can continue to grow with each stage of the infant's development.

Throughout this book, the focus has been on the ways that hypnosis can help an expectant mother develop a strong connection with her baby during pregnancy and childbirth. Thus, hypnosis is not only the means to achieve a comfortable birth, but also an opportunity to create an atmosphere of connectedness between the mother's body and mind, and between the mother herself and the baby. You, the reader, have seen that hypnosis is a powerful way to learn and to teach expectant and new mothers how to consciously develop opportunities for connection with and among individuals. The benefits of hypnosis do not stop with childbirth.

Each mother looks forward to connecting with her baby. She also has her own images and expectations about what this connection means to her and her baby and how best to develop it. Hypnosis is particularly useful for those patients who accept the relational understanding of our day-to-day existence. After all, hypnosis subscribes to the understanding that the activities, thoughts, and words of one person have a specific impact on the people around them. Through hypnosis, our actions are seen in a larger context, as ultimately connected to something else. For example, birth is not perceived as just a biological activity, but as a biological/emotional/social/spiritual activity that is influenced by the expectant mother's beliefs about birthing. It is also conceptualized as an influential force for the relationship that will be established between the mother and the baby and, ultimately, the relationships that will be established between the grown-up baby and his or her children. Therefore, the use of hypnosis during childbirth promotes not only the reliance on the body (and wisdom) welcoming the process of birthing, but also a consideration of the ultimate responsibility of motherhood, in which the choices of the mother and other family members impact the future relational context of the baby.

The understanding of motherhood as a responsible connection also calls for the examination of how the mother can be most present for her child during and after the childbirth. Kabat-Zinn and Kabat-Zinn (1998) point out that "the greatest gift . . . [that the mother] can give [her] child is [herself]" (386). Hypnosis provides the mother an opportunity to offer this gift, since the mother becomes highly aware of her surroundings and is able to welcome the baby as well as establish one of the most welcoming connections for the baby, breastfeeding. Hypnosis also helps the mother stay in touch with her own sensations and emotions, meeting her need to remain a part of the experience. The ability to feel like an active rather than passive participant contributes to the self-worth that positively correlates to the woman's ability to successfully complete baby-related tasks. As a healthcare provider, you also have a choice to participate in the reinforcement of the mother-baby connection by educating your patients on the impact of their influence and engaging them in reflecting on the role that each one of us plays while engaging in diverse interactions. The exploration of what hypnosis brings to the table can serve as a first step toward a gentler birthing and ultimately a more nurturing mothering.

TEN

Conclusion

This book was specifically written for healthcare providers: physicians, nurses, nursing aides, obstetric anesthesiologists, midwives, doulas, and the many other professionals who touch the lives of pregnant women, their families, and their unborn and born babies.

My early professional experience came when I worked as a Medical Family Therapist in a hospice setting, where I was privileged to work side-by-side with physicians, respiratory therapists, nurses, nursing aides, social workers, and chaplains. I witnessed on multiple occasions how a simple touch or a kind word from a physician made a big difference for patients and the whole family and how the caring presence of a nurse helped the family to witness and cope with tragic news. Observing these patient-provider encounters made me realize the incredible influence of healthcare providers' attitudes and words on the well-being of their patients and the patients' loved ones. I noticed that some professionals were able to help their patients to cope better with ailments while others made them worse. It was always important to me to facilitate the communication between healthcare professionals and their patients, giving both sides tools to speak each other's language.

My various professional encounters with medical providers since then have made me realize that current medical education does not always equip healthcare professionals with necessary tools to engage in reflection on their own values, thoughts, and actions. While some professionals find their own way to process their feelings and emotions, others struggle. In addition, a busy medical practice leaves minimal space to address psychosocial-spiritual issues and to explore their own influence, as human beings in addition to their role as medical providers.

My hope is that, having read this book, you will consider how your own presence can make a big difference in patients' lives, and how some unusual techniques can help your patients discover how they would like to relate to themselves and to their future babies.

When citing my previous personal and professional experiences with medical professionals, I always express my gratitude to my healthcare team. They gave me the opportunity to experience the birth that I envisioned. They were there for me, embracing their role as facilitators, not experts. They were true experts in their field. It is important to realize that your patients are often intimidated by medical professionals and by the power emanating from your medical titles. You can acknowledge the inherent imbalance of forces and compensate for it. I believe it is ultimately the healthcare professionals' responsibility to find ways to relate to their patients. Finding the key to the patients' hearts opens new possibilities in the provision of care and facilitates the communication, ultimately providing healthcare professionals with experiences of gratitude and medical compliance.

As you've learned, I hope, hypnosis is one powerful way to establish multiple connections between the body and the mind, feelings and emotions, thoughts and actions, experiences and memories, patients and healthcare professionals. It creates a web that you help to construct, a web that will help the patient cope with multiple circumstances surrounding the pregnancy and childbirth. This web is made of words, thoughtful words, said at the right moments, words that make a big difference and should not be underestimated.

As you noticed, I did not emphasize the need for a formal trance induction. This was intentional. This book is not a manual on how to become a certified hypnotherapist. Rather its purpose is to help you to continue doing what you have probably been doing rather well: relate to your patients, caring for them in your own unique way, continuing to make a difference on a daily basis. It is an additional reminder about the importance of an intentional touch, not only to give the patient a shot, to clean her, or to place an IV, but also because we want to reassure her, to support her, and to comfort her. It is also a reminder that a kind word will remain as a kind mantra throughout the patient's stay in your care and long after she leaves the hospital.

"If I already am doing it, why did I need to read this book," you might ask. Well, if you already have made such a difference in your patients' lives while doing it unintentionally, imagine what you can accomplish if you do it mindfully? This book gives you the tools to do just that, to engage in a mindfulness practice. Remember that, after all, each hypnosis is just self-hypnosis.

Appendix A

Hypnotic Techniques for Healthcare Providers

The following prompts and techniques are intended to help healthcare professionals engage in conversation with their patients at different times during pregnancy, delivery, and postpartum.

PROMPTS FOR A MORE MINDFUL APPROACH TO CARE:

ASK YOURSELF:

- How do my upbringing, my values, and my beliefs about a safe childbirth influence my care for my patients?
- What made me ask this specific question at this specific time?
- Why am I curious to hear this specific story?
- How does what my patient just told me make me feel?

PROMPTS FOR SELF-DISCOVERY AND SELF-EXAMINATION BY EXPECTANT MOTHERS AND THEIR FAMILIES:

- What are your hopes, dreams, and goals as an expectant mother and as a woman in general? What have you planned to achieve but haven't? What makes you sad, happy, proud?
- What does it mean to you to be pregnant? What is your image of a successful pregnancy?
- What does it mean to you to be in labor? How do you envision a successful labor? What do you expect from yourself?
- How do you envision the first encounter with your child? What will it mean to hear your child's first sound, to touch your child, to see your child?
- How will the process of birth affect your first interactions with your child? What will you be able to do, not be able to do?
- How does the environment in which you give birth influence your perceptions and shape your experience? What environment do you envision when you think about giving birth?

- What does the birthing experience tell you about yourself, the family in which you live, the relationships you have with your loved ones?

PROMPTS TO ESTABLISH A SUCCESSFUL BIRTHING PLAN:

- No question is stupid; encourage the patient to ask you any question, even the one that might appear stupid or trivial.
- Do not look at your watch when talking to your client: this is an unusual kind of conversation in a medical world in which each second is precious and to be guarded. Plan the conversation ahead and spend as much time as necessary to answer all the questions. Consider this time as an investment in the trust between you and your patient.
- Do not use medical jargon or fancy technical words. They might make the client shy to ask a question. Try to use the patient's language as much as possible (even the same words) and summarize what your patient says to make sure that you understand her.
- When addressing the Birthing Plan, point out the discrepancy between the fluidity and unpredictability of a birth and a rigid checklist. Engage the patient in a conversation about prioritizing and compromising. Help her to consider the sentences in the plan not as concrete but as drops of rain, the amount of which may vary from creating a puddle or a little river. Some puddles will dry out, while others will expand. Consider talking to a patient about the plan as baby steps toward the unknown and somewhat frightening world of giving birth to another human being.
- Finally, instead of just listening to what an expectant mother does not want to do, help her articulate what she does want. A positive framework can provide your patient with a sense of direction much more effectively than a negative statement that offers no alternative.
- What message would you like to transmit to your child?

PROMPTS TO HELP EXPECTANT MOTHERS TO CREATE THEIR VISIONS OF A SUCCESSFUL BIRTH:

- The Miracle Question (de Shazer and Dolan 2007):

"Try considering a rather strange question. . . . The strange question is this. . . . After you finish reading this sentence, you will go back to your work (home, school) and you will do whatever you need to do the rest of today, such as taking care of the children, cooking dinner, watching TV, giving the children a bath, and so on. . . . It will be time to go to bed [think of specific circumstances that apply to your patient's daily routine]. Everybody in your household is quiet, and you are sleeping in peace. In the middle of the night, a miracle happens, and you are able to envision the birth of your child, as you would like it to happen. . . . But because this happens while you and everyone in your household is sleeping, you have no way of sharing your vision with your loved ones. . . . So, when you wake up tomorrow morning, what do you want to share with everyone in your house (with your loved ones or your birth partner)? . . . What details from your dream will you share with your loved ones? What was happening in it? . . . Who was present? . . . What were they doing? . . . What were you doing? Imagine that you were able to film a little movie of it. . . . Try to describe with as many details as possible specific scenes from the movie."

- "Door to Birth" (England and Horowitz, 1998):

"If there were a secret door to birth, to giving birth, what would it look like? What's behind it, around it, or in front of it? Is anyone in the picture?" (53)

PROMPTS ON HOW TO ENGAGE YOUR PATIENTS IN EXPLORING THEIR BIRTHING ELEMENT:

- Remember that different people experience comfort and relaxation very differently. What is relaxing for one person may not be relaxing for another.
- The expectant mother's element might be constant throughout her life and then change during pregnancy, or even during the time of birth. Encourage her not to be attached to a particular element, but to pay attention to her sensations and what feels comfortable in the moment. For example, for a long time I felt very comfortable in a forest among tall trees. However, as time passed, this image, while still relaxing, did not resonate with me during my pregnancy — probably because it did not involve my physical sensations, which were more prominent when I was immersed in water. I did not try to talk myself into staying with the image of the forest, but instead embraced what felt the most natural at that moment in time.
- The element does not have to evoke or be something that actually happened or is happening. For some women, creating their own image or world is more soothing and beneficial. Others might remember a sensation from the past. I once attended a workshop by well-known psychotherapist Yvonne Dolan. She spoke about a friend who had asked her to help him overcome his fear of flying. Yvonne helped him recreate an image of a very comfortable chair he had once owned. Imagining himself sitting in that chair,

Yvonne's friend felt instantly more relaxed and was able to focus less on his fear of flying.

- Encourage your patients to explore their element with curiosity by paying attention to each specific detail. They can also find ways to compare themselves to a particular element. For example, my mother shared with me that when she was giving birth, she noticed a tree outside that was swaying under the pressure of the wind. She compared her own body to the swaying tree, so that each time she felt contractions, she breathed and moved forward with her body like the tree.

- The more your patients interact with their element, the more familiar they become with it. They then can use this familiarity and the details they conjure in their mind to create their place of comfort. In fact, concentrating on these details and becoming curious about them eventually distracts them from their fears, anxiety, or discomfort.

- Progressive relaxation can help your patients become curious about the sensations in their bodies, examining them part by part, noticing where they feel the most tension and the most relaxation, and watching how these sensations change while they examine them.

- Remember that your patients don't have to have a constant element or stick to only one. They can also explore the surrounding environment, or be captured by certain characteristics of their present experience, and be able to recreate a relaxing or comfortable sensation on the spot.

- Finally, remind your patients that they don't have to make these explorations alone. You can help them find their way or refer them to a qualified hypnotherapist before they continue practicing on their own.

PROMPTS FOR LABOR:

- "Encouraging and Restraining" (O'Hanlon and Martin 1992):

In this, you encourage the woman to experience the future birthing event in a way that is appropriate to her. For example, while you encourage the pregnant woman to practice the techniques, you might tell her that she should only practice them when it feels comfortable and even tell her not to overdo it. Remember, you do not want the woman to expect that a specific practice will produce a specific effect. She will be setting herself up for disappointment. So you might advise her to go slowly and not to over practice, almost as an athlete or a ballet dancer is encouraged to rehearse but not overdo it before the final demonstration of their talent (note that I did not use the word "competition" or "performance"). The future mother is not competing with herself or with another pregnant woman. She is exploring different possibilities rather than rehearsing for a perfect birth. It is important to point out this difference to avoid her disappointment if the birth does not progress "as expected." (It never does.)

PROMPTS TO ASSIST THE MOTHER POSTPARTUM TO EXPLORE THE FAMILY TRANSFORMATION:

- What does it mean for her to be a mother?
- What are her needs? What are the baby's needs? Where do the two overlap? Where do they separate?
- What is the mother doing for herself in order to take the best care of her baby?
- What are the mother's experiences of her interactions with the baby?
- What are her experiences of being a mother?
- What would the mother like to teach her child during the first years of his life?

PROMPTS FOR THE PARTNER:

- How is he/she coping with his/her new role?
- How does he/she perceive his/her position in the new family structure?
- What memories and old emotions are brought up by this new situation?
- How can he/she continue to find and enjoy the little moments with his/her partner?
- How can each of them relax, breathe, connect, and develop?
- How will both parents continue to transform, creating a strong foundation for their new unit?

TECHNIQUES FOR EXPECTANT MOTHERS:

Breathing (HypnoBirthing, Mongan's Method [2005])

- Sleep Breathing

"Draw in a breath from your stomach. To a count of four, mentally recite "In 1–2–3–4"on the intake. Feel your stomach rise as you draw the breath up and into the back of your throat. As you exhale, mentally recite "Out 1–2–3–4–5–6–7–8." Do not exhale through your mouth. As you breath out very slowly through your nose, direct the energy of the breath down and inward toward the back of your throat, allowing your shoulders to droop into the frame of your body" (Mongan 2005, 125). To ensure that you are executing the technique correctly, Mongan continues, "place your left hand on your stomach and your right hand on the lower part of your chest. As you inhale, you should feel your left hand rising as though your stomach were inflating like a balloon. As you exhale, you will feel your hands fold into each other, as your chest and stomach create a crevice" (125).

- Slow Breathing

"Lying in a lateral position, place your hands across the top of your abdomen so that your fingers barely meet. Exhale briefly to clear your lungs and nasal passages. Slowly and gradually draw in your breath to a rapid count from 1 to 20+ as though you were inflating your belly. *Avoid using short intakes of breath* [emphasis the author's]; it can tire you and requires that you take several breaths in order to get through the surge. The slow intake to a rapid count up to 20+ and the equally slow exhalation will allow you sufficient time to work with each surge. If it is necessary for you to take a second breath during a surge, do so in the very same manner. Do not hold your breath—ever. . . . While breathing in, focus your attention on your rising abdomen and bring the surge up as much as you can; visualize filling a balloon inside your abdomen as you draw in. *Slowly* exhale to the same count, breathing downward and outward" (Mongan 2005, 127).

- Birth Breathing

"Close your eyes to avoid tearing the blood vessels in your eyes. Placing the tip of your tongue at the place where your front teeth and palate meet will help your lower jaw to recede so that you remain free of tension in your mouth and jaw area. This also helps relax the vagina outlet. When you feel the onset of a surge, follow it. Take a short, but deep, breath through your nose and direct the energy of that breath to the lower back of your throat and down through your body behind your baby in the form of a "J"—down and forward. Allow the muscles in your vaginal area to open as though you were letting the breath out through them or moving your bowels. Don't ride out or hang on to a breath beyond its effectiveness and don't allow those lower muscles to tighten. Repeat this process to take in another short, deep breath and breathe down in the same pattern as above—and then another" (Mongan 2005, 130).

Relaxation (HypnoBirthing, Mongan's Method [2005])

- Progressive Relaxation: starts in a specific part of the body and progressively moved to other parts.
- Disappearing Letters: patient is envisioning disappearing letters while experiencing a deeper relaxation.

- Light touch massage: might be provided by doula or a patient's partner.
- Anchors: utilization of relaxing situations/images, and the like, to evoke relaxation.

Visualization (HypnoBirthing, Mongan's Method [2005])

- Opening Blossom: likens the cervix to an opening rose
- Blue Satin Ribbons: the cervix is visualized as soft blue satin ribbons
- The Rainbow Relaxation: a guided imagery CD provided in HypnoBirthing

Deepening (HypnoBirthing, Mongan's Method [2005])

- Glove Relaxation: "Imagine that you are putting a soft, silver glove onto your right hand—a special glove of natural endorphins. Immediately, the fingers of your hand begin to feel larger and to tingle, as though there were springs at the ends of your fingers. The silver glove, with its endorphins flowing around your fingers, your palm and the back of your hand will cause your hand to feel numb, the way it would if you were to place it into a large container of icy slush" (152). Once the feeling is acquired in the hand, the patient then can transfer this feeling to different parts of her body, being able to spread the feeling of numbness and comfort.
- The Depthometer: a painful sensation can become lighter and lighter as the woman counts down or up, whichever feels more in line with her sensation.
- Time Distortion: invites the woman to give herself a suggestion that five minutes now seems as only one minute. An expectant mother would first have to bring herself in a state of relaxation and then try this technique. This exercise can also involve the birthing partner, who can provide similar suggestions to the mother in labor.

Appendix B

Foundations of Hypnosis

These guidelines provide an important but not exhaustive foundation for the successful implementation of hypnotic techniques during pregnancy and childbirth.

1: Practice, Practice, Practice

Hypnotic techniques need to be practiced long before the actual birthing day. This way they become second nature and come naturally during the delivery. In addition, practicing hypnotic technique helps future mothers develop coping strategies for the stressors of pregnancy and acquire personalized ways to induce self-hypnosis.

2: Anything that Complements Hypnosis

Nutrition, exercise, birthing position, and a helpful, caring team are as important to a successful birth as any chosen technique.

3: Each Birth Is Different

The messages to the expectant mother need to be, "No one birth is like another," and "Consider what constitutes a special, safe, desirable birth for you."

4: No Question Is a Stupid Question

Encourage your patients to ask you any questions, even those that might seem stupid or naïve. It will open a line of communication that will allow you to explore your patients' understanding of what you are telling them.

5: Explore Your Patient's Comfortable Element

Engage your patient, the future mother, in thinking about her element. After you discover the element that makes her feel comfortable, you can use her connection with it in the different ways I described earlier, as well as in new ways that make sense for her.

Glossary

Biopsychosocial-Spiritual Approach: A systems-based medical approach to the assessment and treatment of physical and mental health conditions that emphasizes the connection between the body, mind, emotions, and spirit.

Birth Breathing: A hypnobirth technique developed by Marie Mongan (2005) that is used during the second stage of labor to help the actual birth of the baby.

Birthing Plan (aka Birth Preference Sheets) (Mongan 2005): A plan made by the expecting mother with her provider that includes specific details pertaining to the birthing process, such as medical interventions unacceptable to her, those who may be with her during the childbirth, and how she wants the infant to be treated in the few seconds after the baby is born (www.americanpregnancy.org/).

Breathing in Hypnobirthing: Hypnobirthing technique developed by Marie Mongan (2005) that encompasses three types of breathing patterns: Sleeping breathing, Slow breathing, and Birth breathing.

Circular Causality: A relational understanding of the world rather than a linear cause-and-effect interpretation of events. When circular causality takes precedence in our interpretations, it allows us to account for multiple possibilities and viewpoints, opening multiple ways to understand and account for a particular phenomenon

Clinical Hypnosis: A set of assessments and techniques used to address and minimize patients' symptoms.

Deepening Technique: A HypnoBirthing technique (Mongan 2005) designed to enhance the efficacy of the Birth Breathing technique. This method helps birthing mothers achieve a very relaxed state that usually lasts until the baby is born.

Doula: An experienced and trained professional who provides physical, emotional, and spiritual support to mothers before, during, and just after birth (www.dona.org/).

Ericksonian Hypnosis: A method of hypnosis that allows access to possibilities through personalized, strength-based utilization.

HypnoBirthing: A method of delivery developed by hypnotherapist Marie Mongan (2005). An overarching philosophy for approaching pregnancy and birthing rather than a specific technique implemented at a particular time during active labor.

Hypnosis: A unique means to connect our mind, body, and spirit to alter our experiences and sensations and understandings.

Hypnotherapy: The use of specific hypnotic techniques in psychotherapy.

Hypnotic Induction: A procedure designed to induce hypnosis (APA, Division 30).

Meditation: The practice of mental focus comprised of a variety of ways, including mindfulness, to relate to our being.

Mindfulness: According to Jon Kabat-Zinn, MD, renowned teacher of mindfulness meditation (2005), "the art of conscious living." The aim of mindfulness is to cultivate our ability to be attentive to every moment, appreciating our life experience as it is and our interconnectedness with the world around us.

Natural Birth: Vaginal birth, with or without the use of pharmaceutical drugs; birth without pain-relieving drugs; birth without any drugs whatsoever; birth with only select interventions allowed, according to the mother's birth plan; birth with the fewest interventions necessary to support the health of the mother and the baby (Gabriel 2011).

Prenatal Classes: Classes to prepare women for their birthing process by teaching them the anatomy and physiology of pregnancy and labor.

Relaxation for HypnoBirth: One of the four techniques in Mongan's Method (2005), which might include progressive relaxation, disappearing letters, light touch massage, and anchors.

Self-Hypnosis: According to Douglas Flemons (2001), similar to the state of inner absorption. Many authors on hypnosis suggest that any experience of hypnosis is an experience of self-hypnosis for the therapist and the client.

Sleep Breathing: A technique in HypnoBirthing (Mongan 2005) that aims to introduce a state of relaxation to optimize such practices as guided imagery and visualization.

Slow Breathing: A technique in HypnoBirthing (Mongan 2005) used specifically during the first stage of labor to stimulate the opening of the cervix and ease contractions (called "waves" in this approach).

Solution-Oriented Therapy (aka Possibilities Therapy): A therapeutic approach based on validation, flexibility, and language precision.

Suggestibility: According to Michael Yapko (1995), "the person's ability to accept new ideas, new information" (37).

Susceptibility: The ability to be influenced by another person. It is part of a successful hypnosis and can be established by the joining between the practitioner and the client.

Systems-Based Thinking: An understanding of the world and events as a complex web of interconnected relationships.

Trance: According to Jay Haley (1993), "that moment of shift when the subject begins to follow suggestions involuntarily" (77).

Visualization: One of the fundamental techniques in HypnoBirthing (Mongan, 2005) and other hypnotic approaches. It is designed to enhance the experience of breathing and relaxation and is mostly utilized in the first stage of labor. This includes the Opening Blossom (which likens the cervix to an opening rose), Blue Satin Ribbons (the cervix is visualized as soft blue satin ribbons), and the arm-wrist relaxation test. The Rainbow relaxation, also included in these visualizations, is not limited to use during labor. The expectant mother is taught to practice this technique every day, following a script and a CD.

Yoga: A practice engaging the body, mind, and spirit. It is built on three main pillars: deep bodily relaxation achieved in different postures (called *asanas*), decreased respiratory rate via controlled slow breathing (called *pranayama*), and mental steadiness reached by techniques such as meditation and chanting.

References

Abbasi, M., Ghazi, F., Barlow-Harrison, A., Sheikhvatan, M., and Mohammadyari, F. (2009). "The Effect of Hypnosis on Pain Relief during Labor and Childbirth in Iranian Pregnant Women." *International Journal of Clinical and Experimental Hypnosis* 57(2), 176–183.

Aceros, J. (2012). "Social Construction and Relationalism: A Conversation with Kenneth Gergen." *Universitas Psychologica* 11(3), 1001–1011.

Arnie , W. R., and Neil, J. (1982). "The Location of Pain in Childbirth: Natural Childbirth and Transformation of Obstetrics." *Sociology of Health and Illness* 4(1), 1–23.

Arya, R., Chansoria, M., Konanki, R., and Tiwari, D. K. (2012). "Maternal Music Exposure during Pregnancy Influences Neonatal Behavior: An Open-Labor Randomized Controlled Trial." *International Journal of Pediatrics* , 1–6.

Bateson, G. (2000). *Steps to an Ecology of Mind.* Chicago, IL: University of Chicago Press.

Bioy, A., and Wood, C. (2006). "Hypnosis: Principles of Use and Benefits in Palliative Care." *European Journal of Palliative Care* 13(3), 117–120.

Brown, D. C., and Hammond, D. C. (2007). "Evidence-Based Clinical Hypnosis for Obstetrics, Labor and Delivery, and Preterm Labor." *International Journal of Clinical and Experimental Hypnosis* 55(3), 355–371.

Browning, C. A. (2000). "Using Music during Childbirth." *Birth* 27(4), 272–276.

Caracappa, J. M. (1963). "Hypnosis and Terminal Cancer." *American Journal of Clinical Hypnosis, 5,* 205–206.

Cerini, C., and Aldrovandi, G. M. (2013). "Breast Milk: Proactive Immunomodulation and Mucosal Protection against Viruses and Other Pathogens." *Future Virology* 8(11), 1127–1134.

Conkling, W. (2002). *Hypnosis for a Joyful Pregnancy and Pain-Free Labor and Delivery.* New York: St. Martin's Griffin.

Curtis, C. (2001). "Hypnotherapy in a Specialist Palliative Care Unit: Evaluation of a Pilot Study." *International Journal of Palliative Nursing* 7(12), 604–609.

Cyna, A. M., & Andrew, M. I. (2006). "Antenatal Self-Hypnosis for Labor and Childbirth: A Pilot Study." *Anesthesia and Intensive Care* 34(4), 464–469.

De Jong, P., and Kim Berg, I. (2012). *Interviewing for Solutions.* Belmont, CA: Cengage.

de Shazer, S. (1985). *Keys to Solution in Brief Therapy.* New York: W. W. Norton & Company.

de Shazer, S. (1988). "Utilization: The Foundation of Solutions." In J. K. Zeig (ed.), *Developing Ericksonian Therapy: State of Art,* 112–124. New York: Brunner/Mazel.

de Shazer, S. (1994). *Words Were Originally Magic.* New York: W. W. Norton & Company.

de Shazer, S., and Dolan, Y. (2007). *More than Miracles: The State of the Art of Solution-Focused Brief Therapy.* New York: Routledge.

Dermer, A. (1998). "Breastfeeding and Women's Health." *Journal of Women's Health* 7(4), 427–433.

Dermer, A. (2001). "A Well-Kept Secret: Breastfeeding's Benefits to Mothers." *New Beginnings* 18(4), 124–127.

Do Carmo França-Botelho, A., Carvalho Ferreira, M., França, J. L., França, E. L., and Honorio-França, A. C. (2012). "Breastfeeding and Its Relationship with Reduction of Breast Cancer: A Review." *Asian Pacific Journal of Cancer Prevention* 13(11), 5327–5332.

Douglas, D. (1999). "Hypnosis: Useful, Neglected, Available." *American Journal of Hospice and Palliative Medicine 16*(5), 665–670.

Ellis, H. (2009). "Grantly Dick-Read: Advocate of Natural Childbirth." *British Journal of Hospital Medicine 70*(6), 355–356.

Embracio, N., Papazian, L., Kantish-Barnes, N., Pochard, F., and Azoulay, E. (2007). "Burnout Syndrome among Critical Care Healthcare Workers." *Current Opinion in Critical Care 13*, 482–488.

Engel, G. L. (1977). "The Need for a New Medical Model: A Challenge for Biomedicine." *Science 196*(4286), 129–136.

England, P., and Horowitz, R. (1998). *Birthing from Within*. Albuquerque, NM: Partera Press.

Erickson, M. H. (1959). "Hypnosis in Painful Terminal Illness." *Journal of the Arkansas Medical Society 56*(2), 67–71.

Flemons, D. G. (2001). *Of One Mind: The Logic of Hypnosis, the Practice of Therapy*. New York: W. W. Norton and Company.

Flemons, D. G. (2004). "Embodying the Mind and Minding the Body: Using Hypnosis in Brief Therapy." In S. Madigan (ed.), *Therapeutic Conversations 5: Therapy from Outside In*, 41–53. Vancouver, Canada: Yaletown Family Therapy.

Flemons, D. G., and Wright, K. (1999). "Many Lives, Many Traumas: The Hypnotic Construction of Memory." In W. J. Matthews and J. H. Edgette (eds.), *Current Thinking and Research in Brief Therapy*, vol. 3, 179–195. Philadelphia: Taylor & Francis.

Gabriel, C. (2011). *Natural Hospital Birth: The Best of Both Worlds*. New York: Harvard Common Press.

Gaskin, I. M. (2003). *Ina May's Guide to Childbirth*. New York: Bantam Dell.

Gawain, S. (2002). *Creative Visualization*. Novato, CA: New World Library.

Gedde-Dahl, M., and Fors, E. A., (2011). "Impact of Self-Administered Relaxation and Guided Imagery Techniques during Final Trimester and Birth." *Complementary Therapy in Clinical Practice 18*(1), 6–65.

Gergen, K. J. (2009). *An Invitation to Social Construction*. Thousand Oaks, CA: Sage.

Gilligan, S. G. (1987). *Therapeutic Trances: The Cooperation Principle in Ericksonian Hypnotherapy*. New York: Bruner and Mazel.

Goer, H. (1999). *The Thinking Woman's Guide to a Better Birth*. New York: Perigee Trade.

Green, J. P., Laurence, J-R., and Lynn, S. J. (2014). "Hypnosis and Psychotherapy: From Messmer to Mindfulness." *Psychology of Consciousness: Theory, Research, and Practice 1*(2), 199–212.

Haley, J. (1993). *Uncommon Therapy: The Psychiatric Techniques of Milton H. Erickson*. New York: Norton & Norton Company.

Hildingsson, I. (2012). "Mental Training during Pregnancy: Feelings and Experiences during Pregnancy and Birth and Parental Stress 1 Year after Birth—A Pilot Study." *Sexual and Reproductive Healthcare 3*(1), 31–36.

Hodgson, J., Lamson, A., Mendenhall, T., and Crane, D. (2014). *Medical Family Therapy: Advanced Applications*. New York: Springer.

Iglesias, A. (2004). "Hypnosis and Existential Psychotherapy with End-Stage Terminally Ill Patients." *American Journal of Clinical Hypnosis 46*(3), 201–213.

Jallo, N., Cozens, R., Smith, M. W., and Simpson, R. I. (2013). "Effects of a Guided Imagery Intervention on Stress in Hospitalized Pregnant Women: A Pilot Study." *Holistic Nursing Practitioner 27*(3), 129–139.

Jones, J. C. (2012). "Idealized and Industrialized Labor: Anatomy of Feminist Controversy." *Hypatia 27*(1), 99–117.

Jones, L., Othman, M., Dowswell, T., Alfirevic, Z., Gates, S., Newburn, M. . . . Neilson, J. P. (2012). "Pain Management for Women in Labor: An Overview of Systematic Reviews." *Cochrane Database of Systematic Reviews 3*. Retrieved from www.scienceandsensibility.org/?p=4363.

Kabat-Zinn, J. (2005). *Wherever You Go, There You Are*. New York: MJF Books.

Kabat-Zinn, M., and Kabat-Zinn, J. (1998). *Everyday Blessings: The Inner Work of Mindful Parenting*. New York: Hyperion.

Karmel, M. (2005). *Thank You, Dr. Lamaze*. London, UK: Pinter and Martin.

Karp, H. (2003). *The Happiest Baby on the Block*. New York: Bantam.

Kearney, M. K., Weininger, B. B., Vachon, M. L. S., Harrison, B. L., and Mount, B. M. (2009). "Self-Care of Physicians Caring for Patients at the End of Life. Being Connected . . . A Key to My Survival." *JAMA 301*(11), 1155–1164.

Keeney, B. (2002). *Aesthetics of Change*. New York: The Guilford Press.

Kerr, M., and Bowen, M. (1988). *Family Evaluation*. New York: W. W. Norton and Company.

Kuhn, T. S. (1962). *The Structure of Scientific Revolutions*. Chicago, IL: University of Chicago Press.

Lindbergh, A. M. (2005). *Gift from the Sea*. New York: Pantheon Books.

Little, M., Lyerly, A., Mitchell. L., Armstrong, E., Harris, L., Kukla, R., and Kupperman, M. (2008). "Mode of Delivery: Toward Responsible Inclusion of Patient Preferences." *Obstetrics and Gynecology 113*(1), 230–231.

Lowe, R. H., and Frey, J. D. (1983). "Predicting Lamaze Childbirth Intentions and Outcomes: An Extension of the Theory of Reasoned Action to a Joint Outcome." *Basic and Applied Social Psychology 4*(4), 353–372.

Lynn, S. J., and Rhue, J. W. (eds.). (1991). *Theories of Hypnosis: Current Models and Perspectives*. New York: Guilford Press.

Marino, K. (2009). *Pain Management*. Paper presented at the in-service of Douglas Gardens Hospice, Miami, FL.

McManus, A. J., Hunter, L. P., and Renn, H. (2006). "Lesbian Experiences and Needs during Childbirth: Guidance for Healthcare Providers." *Journal of Obstetrical Gynecological Neonatal Nursing 35*(1), 13–23.

Mehl-Madrona, L. (2004). "Hypnosis to Facilitate Uncomplicated Birth." *American Journal of Clinical Hypnosis 46*(4), 299–312.

Miller, A. C., and Shriver, T. E. (2012). "Women's Childbirth Preferences and Practices in the United States." *Social Science and Medicine 75*(4), 709–716.

Molyneaux, B. T. (2013). *Hypnosis for Breastfeeding*. MP3.

Mongan, M. F. (2005). *HypnoBirthing: The Mongan Method*. Deerfield Beach, FL: Health Communications.

Nabb, M. T., Kimber, L., Haines, A., and McCourt, C. (2006). "Does Regular Massage from Late Pregnancy to Birth Decrease Maternal Pain Perception during Labor and Birth?—A Feasibility Study to Investigate a Program of Massage, Controlled Breathing, and Visualization from 36 Weeks Pregnancy until Birth." *Complementary Therapies in Clinical Practice 12*, 222–231.

Narendran, S., Nagarathna, R., Narendran, V., Gunasheela, S., and Nagendra, H. R. R. (2005). "Efficacy of Yoga on Pregnancy Outcome." *The Journal of Alternative and Complementary Medicine 11*(2): 237–244.

Novak, D. H., Epstein, R. M., and Paulsen, R. H. (1999). "Toward Creating Physicians-Healers: Fostering Medical Students' Self-Awareness, Personal Growth, and Well-Being." *Academic Medicine 74*(5), 516–520.

O'Hanlon, B., and Wilk, J. (1987). *Contexts: The Generation of Effective Psychotherapy*. New York: Guilford Press.

O'Hanlon, W. H., and Martin, M. (1992). *Solution-Oriented Hypnosis: An Ericksonian Approach*. New York: W. W. Norton & Company.

Pan, C. X., Morrison, R. S., Ness, J., and Fugh-Berman, R. M. (2000). "Complementary and Alternative Medicine in the Management of Pain, Dyspnea, and Nausea and Vomiting near the End of Life. A Systematic Review." *Journal of Pain and Symptom Management, 20*(5), 374–387.

Pastor Montero, S. M., Romero Sanchez, H. M., and Hueso Montoro, C. (2011). "Experiences with Perinatal Loss from the Health Professional's Perspective." *Revista Latino-Americana de enfermagem 19*(6), 1405–1412.

Peter, B. (2005). "Gassner's Exorcism not Messmer's Magnetism Is the Real Predecessor of Modern Hypnosis." *International Journal of Clinical and Experimental Hypnosis 53*(1), 1–12.

Poreba, A., Dudkiewicz, D., and Drygalski, M. (2000). "The Influence of the Sounds of Music on Chosen Cardiotocographic Parameters in Mature Pregnancies." *Ginekologia Polska 71*(8), 915–920.

Rabet, L. M., Vos, A. P., Boehm, G., and Garssen, J. (2008). "Breastfeeding and Its Role in Early Development of the Immune System in Infants: Consequences for Health Later in Life." *Journal of Nutrition 138*(9), 1782–1790.

Rajasekaran, M., Edmonds, P. M., and Higginson, I. L. (2005). "Systematic Review of Hypnotherapy for Treating Symptoms in Terminally Ill Adult Cancer Patients." *Palliative Medicine 19*(5), 418–426.

Rajasekaran, M., Edmonds, P. M., and Higginson, I. L. (2010). "Evidence, Ontology, and Psychological Science: The Lesson of Hypnosis." *Journal of Theoretical and Philosophical Psychology 30*(1), 51–65.

Ryding, E. L., Wijma, B., and Wijma, K. (1997). "Posttraumatic Stress Reactions after Emergency Cesarean Section." *Acta Obstetricia et Gynecologica Scandinavica 76*(9), 856–861.

Schaal, B., Marlier, L., and Soussignan, R. (2000). "Human Fetuses Learn Odors from Their Pregnant Mother's Diet." *Chemical Senses 25*(6), 729–737.

Sears, M., and Sears, W. (2000). *The Breastfeeding Book.* New York: Little, Brown, and Company.

Sears, W., and Sears, M. (1994). *The Birth Book.* New York: Little, Brown, and Company.

Sears, W., Sears, M., Sears, R., and Sears, J. (2013). *The Baby Book.* New York: Little, Brown, and Company.

Shi, L., and Singh, D. A. (2008). *Delivering Health Care in America: A Systems Approach.* Sudbury, MA: Jones and Bartlett Publishers.

Simkin, P. (2008). *The Birth Partner.* Boston: The Harvard Common Press.

Stone, E. (2002). *A Boy I Once Knew: What a Teacher Learned from Her Student.* Chapel Hill, NC: Algonquin Books of Chapel Hill.

Sun, Y.-C., Hung, Y.-C., Chung, Y., and Kuo, S.-C. (2010). "Effects of a Prenatal Yoga Program on the Discomforts of Pregnancy and Maternal Childbirth Efficacy in Taiwan." *Midwifery 26*(6), 31–36.

Van Teijlingen, E. R., Wrede, S., Benoit, C., Sandall, J., and DeVries, R. (2009). "Born in the USA: Exceptionalism in the Maternity Care Organization among High-Income Countries." *Sociological Research Online* 14(1). Retrieved from www.socresonline.org.uk/14/1/5.html.

Werner, A., Uldbjerg, N., Zacariae, R., Rosen, G., and Nohr, E. A. (2012). "Self-Hypnosis for Coping with Labor Pain: A Randomized Controlled Trial." *International Journal of Obstetrics and Gynecology 120*(3), 346–353.

Willard, R. D. (1974). "Perpetual Trance as a Means of Controlling Pain in the Treatment of Terminal Cancer with Hypnosis." *The Journal of the American Institute of Hypnosis 15*, 111–131.

Wittgenstein, L. (2001). *Philosophical Investigations.* Malden, MA: Blackwell Publishing.

World Health Organization (2014). *Breastfeeding.* Retrieved from www.who.int/topics/breastfeeding/en/.

Yapko, M. (1995). *Essentials of Hypnosis.* Levittown, PA: Brunner/Mazel.

Zeig, J. K. (1980). *A Teaching Seminar with Milton Erickson, M.D.* New York: Brunner/Mazel.

Zeig, J. K. (1994). "Advanced Techniques of Utilization." In J. K. Zeig (ed.), *Ericksonian Methods: The Essence of the Story*, 295–314. New York: Brunner/Mazel.

Zeig, J. K. (2006). *Confluences: The Selected Papers of Jeffrey Zeig.* Phoenix, AZ: Tucker & Theisen.

Index

American Pregnancy Association,
43–44
American Society of Clinical Hypnosis,
3
anchoring technique, 37–38
anesthesia, 23, 33, 79
animal magnetism, 2
Association of American
Psychoprophylactic Obstetrics
(ASPO), 23
associations, with birth, xx, xxi
automatism, 2

Bateson, Gregory, 5, 33, 67
Bernheim, Hippolyte, 2–3
biological advantages, of
breastfeeding, 94–95
biopsychosocial-spiritual approach, 5,
32, 111
birth: about, xix–xxii; associations
with, xx, xxi; experiences of, xx,
72–73, 74–76, 89; options about, 46;
unexpected changes with, 75; in
water, 55. *See also* natural birth
birth, life after, 91; first breastfeeding,
94–96; motherhood, 97; new family,
91–94
birth breathing, 59, 106, 111
birthing element, 103–104
birthing process, xxi–xxii
birthing views, of Mongan, 26–27, 34,
35, 48, 62, 75
Birth Plan, 43–45, 87, 102, 111
"Birth Preference Sheets", 43
bodies. *See* minds, bodies, spirits
A Boy I Once Knew (Stone), 97
Braid, James, 2
breastfeeding, 94; biological
advantages of, 94–95; connections
with, 94, 94–95, 96; issues with, 95;

physiological benefits of, 94;
techniques of, 96
breathing: birth, 59, 106, 111;
controlled, 76, 87; exercises for, 56;
in hypnobirthing, 111; hypnotic
essentials and, 56–59; patterns of,
57, 58, 59; practice of, 54; sleep,
57–58, 105–106, 112; slow, 58–59,
106, 112; for trance, 57

caregivers, 74–75; hypnosis with, xv;
needs of, 89–90; professional, 88–90;
self-care among, 89
Center of Mindfulness in Medicine,
Health Care, and Society, 89
child. *See* mother and child
childbirth: culture of, 24–26, 33, 40;
hypnobirth history, 26–29; language
with, 39, 44–45; natural childbirth
history, 21–26; practices of, 24–26;
pregnancy and, 21; support during,
41; tradition relating to, 40;
transitional time of, 39–40. *See also*
social childbirth philosophy
Childbirth without Fear (Dick-Read), 23
chloroform, 22
circular causality, 31, 31–32, 111
classes: for HypnoBirthing, 27, 48, 50,
63; prenatal, 112
clinical hypnosis, 13, 111
communication, hypnosis and, 6
conceptualizations, of hypnosis,
xviii–xix, 4–5, 9
connections: with breastfeeding, 94,
94–95, 96; hypnosis with, 31, 85;
minds, bodies, spirits, 31–34;
mother and child, 35–36; of new
family, 94; of physician and patient,
32
contractions, pre-labor, 71

mother and child relating to, 37–38;
optimal surroundings for, 19;
perceptions about, xx; philosophy
of, xxii; possibilities of, xvi;
practitioners and, xv; providers
and, xv; psychotherapy and, 17;
qualifications for, 20; relational, 11;
self-hypnosis, 17, 112; sessions of,
19–20; why's and how's of,
xxii–xxiii. *See also* Ericksonian
hypnosis
Hypnosis and Suggestibility (Hull), 3
hypnosis myths, xv, xvi, xvii, 12–13, 76;
hypnosis as part of natural birth,
15–16; hypnosis is last resort, 13–14;
hypnosis is sleep or relaxation,
14–15; memory recall, 15; mind
control, 14; special environment for
trance, 14; stuck in hypnotic state,
14
hypnotherapy, 12, 17, 34, 82, 112
hypnotic aids, 61; music, 67–69;
visualization, 61–64, 85–86, 87, 113;
yoga, 47, 64–67, 113
hypnotic assistance, in unexpected, 81;
with C-section, 86; for future
mothers, 86–87; with partners,
87–88; with professional caregivers,
88–90; symptom management,
82–86
hypnotic essentials, 53; breathing,
56–59; elements of, 53–56; water as,
53–55
hypnotic induction, 16, 112
hypnotic mindset, 39; plan, 42–45;
teambuilding, 46–50; vision, 39–42
hypnotic phenomenon, 3, 5
hypnotic state, 14
hypnotic techniques, for healthcare
providers, 101–107

imagination, with visualization, 62
The Inner Work of Mindful Parenting
(Kabat-Zinn and Kabat-Zinn), 35

Janet, Pierre, 2

Kabat-Zinn, Jon, 17, 35, 36–37, 39, 87
Kabat-Zinn, M., 35, 36–37, 39

Kuhn, Thomas, 3

labor, xxi, 22; fear during, 23, 80; pain
during, 83; progression of, 77;
prompts for, 104; timeline of, 78
Lamaze, Ferdinand, 23–24
language: with childbirth, 39, 44–45;
precise, 10, 11
Lindbergh, Anne Morrow, 53–54
Lull, Clifford, 23

management: hypnosis and, 82–86; of
pain, 22, 82
Medical Family Therapist, 99
medical science, hypnosis and, 2
meditation, 18, 56, 112
mediumship, 2
memory recall, 15
Messmer, Franz Anton, 1–2
Milton Erickson Foundation, 10
mind: control of, 14; unconscious, 6
mindfulness, 17, 56–57, 89, 112
minds, bodies, spirits, 80; connections
of, 31–34; culture relating to, 33;
hypnotherapy relating to, 34
mindset. *See* hypnotic mindset
Miracle Question, 42, 62
modalities combined, 77
Mongan, Marie: anchoring technique
of, 37–38; birthing views of, 26–27,
34, 35, 48, 62, 75; Birth Reference
Sheets of, 43; breathing patterns of,
57, 58, 59; *HypnoBirthing: The
Mongan Method* by, 26, 57, 62, 74, 78,
79
mother and child: connection of, 35–36;
disconnection of, 35; hypnosis
relating to, 37–38; values and beliefs
relating to, 36–37
motherhood, 97
mothers: future, 86–87; postpartum,
105. *See also* expectant mothers
movement, of hypnobirth, xxii
music, 74, 76; as hypnotic aid, 67–69;
responses to, 67–68; selection of,
68–69; use of, 69; utilization of, 68
myths. *See* hypnosis myths

subconscious, 2
suggestibility, 18, 112
support, during childbirth, 41
susceptibility, 18–19, 112
symptom management, hypnosis and,
  82–86
systems-based thinking, 31–32, 33, 112

teambuilding, 46; doula, 47–49;
  helpers, 50; partner, 49–50, 78;
  physician, 46–47
techniques, 101–107, 105; anchoring,
  37–38; birth breathing, 59, 106, 111;
  of breastfeeding, 96; deepening, 28,
  107, 111; encouraging and
  restraining, 73; Glove Relaxation,
  79; for healthcare providers,
  101–107; for hypnobirth, 76–80; of
  HypnoBirthing, 27–28, 74–75; for
  new family, 93; practice of, 71, 73;
  sleep breathing, 57–58, 105–106, 112;
  slow breathing, 58–59, 106, 112;
  Time Distortion, 79–80; trance-
  inducing, 41–42; visualization, 107.
  See also relaxation
therapy: hypnotherapy, 12, 17, 34, 82,
  112; Solution-Oriented, 9–10, 112.
  See also psychotherapy, hypnosis
  and
Time Distortion, 79–80
timeline, of labor, 78
tradition, childbirth relating to, 40
trance, 16–17, 112; breathing for, 57;
  special environment for, 14; state of,
  xviii
trance-inducing techniques, 41–42
transitional time, of childbirth, 39–40

traumatic birth experiences, 89

unconscious mind, Ericksonian
  hypnosis and, 6
unexpected: birth with, 75; hypnotic
  assistance in, 81–90
utilization, 6–8, 68, 82–83

validation, 9
values and beliefs, 36–37
visualization, 76, 77–78; Ericksonian
  hypnosis and, 62; guided imagery
  with, 63; as hypnotic aid, 61–64,
  85–86, 87, 113; imagination with, 62;
  of outcome, 61–64; techniques of,
  107
von Bertalanffy, Ludwig, 32, 33

water: birth in, 55; as hypnotic
  essentials, 53–55
Weiss, Paul, 32, 33
words: list of, 78; power of, 81
World Health Organization, 94

Yapko, Michael, 13
yoga: experiences of, 66–67, 77;
  Hinduism and, 65; as hypnotic aid,
  47, 64–67, 113; practice of, 64;
  prenatal, 64–67; three pillars of, 64
Yoga Sutras (Patanjali), 64

Zeig, Jeffrey, 8–9, 10; approaches of, 11;
  postures relating to, 10; precise
  language and, 11

About the Author

Yulia Watters, PhD, LMFT, is originally from Russia. She completed her Bachelor's degree in psychology in Geneva, Switzerland, and then her Master's and Doctoral degrees in Marriage and Family Therapy at Nova Southeastern University, Fort Lauderdale, FL. Currently, she teaches, supervises, and serves as the Director of Curriculum Development in the School of Marriage and Family Sciences at Northcentral University. She is a clinical member and approved supervisor of the American Association for Marriage and Family Therapy. Dr. Watters also serves on the editorial board of *The Qualitative Report*, a peer-reviewed journal dedicated to a better understanding and practice of qualitative research methods.

As a clinician, she has worked in a variety of settings, including private practice, foster homes, hospitals, and nursing homes. She is also a passionate researcher and has served as research coordinator at the Duke Healthcare Systems Cancer Patients Support Program. She has delivered many lectures and presentations for prestigious organizations, including the annual conferences of the Association for the Behavioral Sciences and Medical Education, the National Council on Aging, the American Association for Marriage and Family Therapy, and the World Family Therapy Congress of the International Family Therapy Association.

Dr. Watters is published in a variety of journals, including *Annals of Behavioral Science and Medical Education, International Journal of Transgenderism, SAGE Research Methods Cases Project, Journal of Sexual and Relational Therapy*, and *Journal of Marital and Family Therapy*. In addition, she has co-authored book chapters related to medical family therapy theories and practice.

Dr. Watters maintains a private practice in Miami, FL, serving a diverse population by providing therapy in three languages: English, French, and Russian.

CPSIA information can be obtained at www.ICGtesting.com
Printed in the USA
BVOW03*1610120215

387416BV00001B/2/P